"The thing I have always loved about Jon is that everything he does is filled with passion, love, creativity, and fun. He approaches cooking like that—as well as his family—and it shines through in the way he and Amelia raise their wonderful kids. This book is not only a recipe book for families, but a story about how their travels and love have shaped their family. It will inspire you to share in their passion and experience their journey."

—**Chef Michael Symon**, James Beard Foundation Award–winning American chef, restaurateur, television personality, and author

NOODLE KIDS

Around the World in
50 Fun, Healthy, Creative
Recipes the Whole Family
Can Cook Together

Jonathon Sawyer

Bookmobile
Fountaindale Public Library
Bolingbrook, IL
(630) 759-2102

Quarry Books
100 Cummings Center, Suite 406L
Beverly, MA 01915

quarrybooks.com • quarryspoon.com

First published in the United States of America in 2015 by
Quarry Books, a member of
Quarto Publishing Group USA Inc.
100 Cummings Center
Suite 406-L
Beverly, Massachusetts 01915-6101
Telephone: (978) 282-9590
Fax: (978) 283-2742
www.quarrybooks.com
Visit www.QuarrySPOON.com and help us celebrate food and culture one spoonful at a time!

10 9 8 7 6 5 4 3 2

ISBN: 978-1-59253-963-5

Digital edition published in 2015
eISBN: 978-1-62788-204-0

Library of Congress Cataloging-in-Publication Data
Sawyer, Jonathon.
  Noodle kids : around the world in 50 fun, healthy, creative recipes the whole family will love / Jonathon Sawyer.
       pages cm
  Summary: "Oodles and oodles of noodles! Get your kids in the kitchen with Noodle Kids. Packed with recipes, tips, suggestions, and inspiration to introduce children to, and get them involved in, making noodles like Japanese ramen, Italian spaghetti, Southeast Asian stir-fires, and classic American mac and cheese. See where these worldly noodle recipes will take you!"
-- Provided by publisher.
  ISBN 978-1-59253-963-5 (paperback) -- ISBN 978-1-62788-204-0 (eISBN)
  1. Noodles. 2. Pasta products. I. Title.
  TX809.N65S39 2015
  641.82'2--dc23
                                                                          2014024878

Writing Assistant: April White
Design: Laura Mcfadden Design, Inc
All photography by Kate Lewis, www.kk-lewis.com, with the exception of the following:
© GODONG/BSIP/agefotostock.com, 129
© David Grossman/alamy.com, 35
© Image Republic Inc./alamy.com, 109
© LOOK Die Bildagentur der Fotografen GmbH/alamy.com, 27; 53
Gary Moss Photography/gettyimages.com, 63
© Frances Roberts/alamy.com, 105
Shutterstock.com, 15; 21; 73

Printed in China

Dedication

To my grandmothers and great-grandmothers for my earliest taste memories, which instilled in me a great appreciation for Eastern European traditions and old-school frugality. To my mom, whose love of food and family inspired me. To my dad—and the ham and cheese sandwich he was enjoying while I was being born—when holding me for the first time, the mayonnaise from his sandwich dripped onto my newborn forehead marking me with an adoration for food. To our animals: Bunny, Bear, Squid, Trout, Alexia, Zane, Vito, and Potato, the best composting mechanism I know. To my kids, Catcher and Louisiana—their constant curiosity continues to drive me to teach, learn, and experience more—your existence makes my life make sense. Amelia, my best friend, wife, and guiding light, who puts up with me and pushes me—I love you.

Contents

Chapter 1

Noodling Around with Noodle Kids

People often ask Amelia and me how we get the kids to eat so well. What is our trick? Well, there is no trick. We talk to the kids about food. We ask questions and engage them in conversations about food. We eat with them. We cook with them. In the kitchen and out, we're Team Sawyer: Catcher, Lulu, Amelia, and the chef—that's me, Jonathon.

Good food is our life. Amelia and I are in the restaurant business. We are fortunate enough to own and run a few of them in Cleveland: The Greenhouse Tavern, Trentina, Sawyer's Street Frites, and Noodlecat, where we serve an awesome mash-up of Japanese-American noodle dishes that have inspired some of the recipes in this book.

Meet the Original Noodle Kids

Catcher is the older of my two kids; he's eight. His name was inspired by the book, *Catcher in the Rye*. Right now Catcher is super into tennis, LEGOS, reading, and math. He was also just recently cast as Tiny Tim in A *Christmas Carol* at Playhouse Square here in Cleveland.

Louisiana, my youngest, is six. She's named after her grand-mothers, Louisa and Anna, and we usually call her Lulu. Lulu is a free spirit who has never cut her hair and recently acted in her first short film. She is very into ballet and cheerleading.

They both like to help me cook.

My wife, Amelia, and I have always thought a lot about cooking for and with our kids. Before Catcher was born, he was diagnosed with a kidney disorder that meant he would have only one working kidney. I'm happy to report that he's fine and leads a pretty normal life, but that was a scary time. We thought a lot about how we would raise kids who were as healthy as possible. We knew it would be important to teach our kids about good food. Catcher and Lulu have grown up visiting me in our restaurants. We love to go to the farm, or the dairy, or the farmers' market together, too. We pick our own apples and tap sugar maple trees for syrup. We eat at local restaurants as a family. Lulu's first solid food was pig ear

Lulu in the kitchen

and Catcher will tell you that Lake Erie smelts are his favorite food. We all have fun on these adventures, and the kids learn where their food comes from.

My kids are pretty open-minded when it comes to food. They are each into, basically, everything that the other one hates. That's the phase we're going through right now. If Louisiana is in love with broccoli today, Catcher doesn't like it. If Catcher is in love with asparagus, Louisiana doesn't like it. Thankfully, both kids like noodles. They are the original Noodle Kids.

Hi. I'm Noodlecat. I'm going on a noodle adventure with the chef. You can come. We're going to eat lots of noodles: stuffed noodles; saucy noodles; ooey, gooey, cheesy noodles; and the most *slurpalicious* ramen in the entire world. Follow me through the book. Any time you spot me, I'll tell you a noodle-y secret. Let's go!

noodlecat

Catcher in the kitchen

Cooking with Kids

Amelia and I have been cooking with Catcher and Lulu since they were old enough to hold up their heads. Lulu's really into cooking right now. She's the ultimate helper in the kitchen. She'll measure out recipes, set up the cutting board, find the rolling pin, and even empty the dishwasher.

Catcher likes cooking, too, but he's more of a typical kid about it. He's only going to do it if it's a fun project—one that takes less than 15 minutes. I should say he likes the *idea* of cooking, but his attention span is finite.

That's the first thing to remember when you are cooking with your kids: They are still your kids. They bring their own personalities to the kitchen.

Amelia, Catcher, Lulu, and Jonathon eating dinner

Tip 1 Cater to your kids' personalities in the kitchen.

Lulu likes cooking for the family. She loves the steps and process behind making a pan of lasagna to share with everyone. Catcher is more interested in personalizing his own dish. He likes to create his own unique bowl of ramen or a special meatball with exactly the ingredients he likes best.

It was Catcher who inspired the first kids' cooking events I hosted. Whenever he came to work with me, Catcher would call playing in the kitchen "cook chefn'." Never "cooking with Dad" or something simple. Always "cook chefn'." So, that's what we called the cooking events we held. During those first few events, we offered the kids fifteen or twenty different pizza toppings—including lots of things they had never tried before—and let them create their own pizzas. It's easy to convince kids to try something new when they have picked it or made it themselves.

Tip 2 The closer your kids are to the food, the more likely they are to eat it.

I learned that lesson when we took Catcher and Lulu to meet farmer Lee Jones for the first time. He's a wonderful farmer out here in Ohio, and he let the kids into the white asparagus tunnels. White asparagus grows in the dark and the kids loved the dim tunnels with white asparagus shooting up everywhere. They picked giant bushels of white asparagus. They had never really loved asparagus before, but when we got home, they gorged themselves on white asparagus.

When I opened our restaurant Noodlecat in Cleveland, we knew we wanted to hold more kids' cooking events. The name was easy: Noodle Kids. During those events, we give the kids dozens and dozens of ingredients to choose from to create their own bowl of ramen. Sometimes there are ingredients, such as tare and tamari, that even their parents have never tried. Or there will be an ingredient that looks unfamiliar because we have prepared it to look more fun to the kids.

We cut kale very finely and blanch it quickly so it tastes more like spinach. There's only one rule when the kids are making ramen: You have to pick two vegetables.

Tip 3 Let your kids choose new things to try.

If a kid is a Noodle Kids regular, I might try to encourage her to sample an unusual ingredient such as fermented tofu or a cool combination such as peanut butter and miso. But if there are kids who've never even tried ramen before, I let them choose anything—as long as there are two vegetables. Vegetables are your friend, I tell them, and this is part of the fun game all these other kids are a part of. Plus, there's a gong in the restaurant you can bang when you make a bowl of ramen with at least two vegetables.

Noodles for breakfast? Yes! Kids do it every day in Vietnam. They eat long, thin, tangly noodles called *pho* with chopsticks, and then slurp up the soup broth just like you—or a sneaky cat—drink the milk from your cereal bowl.

noodlecat

Sometimes a kid will surprise his parents by loving ingredients they've never even consider buying. If it were me, I would definitely add those items to the shopping list and pick them up the next time I was at the grocery store or market.

Tip 4 Make food your family likes.

When Lulu was very young, we discovered she loved clams. She ate a whole plate of them and practically licked it clean. We thought it might be a fluke, so we encouraged her to try them again. She still loved them and now her favorite pasta and clam dish is a regular on our dinner table. (Find the recipe on page 80.)

The kids love all kinds of pasta. They would eat it for breakfast if I let them—and sometimes I do. That's part of what I mean when I say, "Make food your family likes." If there's some ragù Bolognese left over, why not have spaghetti in the morning? (Ragù Bolognese is Catcher's favorite. The recipe for Catcher's Italian Meat Sauce is on page 69.) I also mean that you should tailor recipes to your family's tastes and dietary restrictions—even if a famous chef wrote the recipe. There are many examples of this: If you are allergic to wheat, substitute rice noodles; if your family doesn't like cilantro, try parsley or basil!

Think of cooking for your family as if you were throwing a dinner party every night: You want to make food that everyone will enjoy. And you don't want to stress out too much as the host. You always hear that you should never try out a brand-new recipe at a dinner party, and the same is true of a family cooking project. If you are going to have a ravioli party, make sure you've practiced making ravioli and have a plan for teaching your kids. (A ravioli party is one of Team Sawyer's favorites. See our plan on page 38.)

Tip 5 Have a plan.

The plan is the most important part of any recipe you make with your kids. You want them to be successful in the kitchen. You'll start by giving them simple tasks such as collecting some of the pans or ingredients you need. As they become more confident cooks, you can start teaching them things such as knife skills. I started Catcher and Lulu with tofu and steak knives. You can graduate your kids from a steak knife to a dull paring knife to a sharp paring knife until you have proper sous chefs. It's a goal-oriented process and my kids like knowing that if they learn to dice tofu for soup they can help with slicing the snap peas next. Catcher and Lulu have their own small cutting boards and their own knives. And in our kitchen, they have their own work space because I know they are going to make a mess.

Tip 6 Make a mess.

Making a mess is part of the fun, especially when playing with dough and flour to make different pasta shapes. As a professional chef, I'm a stickler for cleanliness. I wipe my knife down after each cut. I flip the cutting board. I wipe the counter down. It's just a habit. But if the kids have their own space to work on their own projects while you do the real work of getting dinner on the table for the whole family, it doesn't really matter that they get nearly as much ravioli filling on the counter as in the pasta the first time they try. You can clean it up in one swoop after you've all enjoyed dinner. They are having fun.

Tip 7 Always have fun.

Noodlecat Around the World

Who invented the noodle? Who knows for sure? A lot of people think it was the Chinese. (Scientists dug up some really old leftover noodles there.) Other people think it was the Italians. And still others give credit to Arab cooks.

There's even one legend that says that the adventurer Marco Polo (Marco! Polo!) brought noodles from China to Italy and North Africa. It's probably not a true story because there's evidence that the Italians were slurping noodles before that, but it's fun to think about pasta being "discovered" by an adventurer.

Since noodles were invented thousands and thousands of years ago, they've been traveling around the world. People on almost every continent have their own special types of noodles made with the ingredients available to them and cooked with the flavors they like best.

Follow me as I take you on a tour of the world's noodles, from Italy and China to Greece, Korea, and Morocco. It's a tour of spaghetti and ramen and *pastitsio*, *galets*, and couscous. Come on! It'll be delicious.

2

Know Your Noodles

Noodles are a staple—and not just in the Sawyer household. Archeologists say that we've been eating noodles for at least 4,000 years. And nearly every culture around the world, from Italy and Japan to Poland and Afghanistan, has some version of the noodle.

At its most basic, a noodle is unleavened dough, just a combination of some sort of flour and water. From there we dress it up, adding ingredients to the dough or cutting it into fancy shapes or serving it with a favorite sauce.

Noodles can tell a story about the places they come from. Are they cooked during a special holiday? What type of flour is used? How is the dough mixed? How are the noodles shaped?

Some of Our Favorite Noodles

Noodles can be purchase fresh, frozen, or dried. Some are better fresh or fresh-frozen; others, such as bucatini or fregola, are meant to be dried before using. The other option, of course, is making the noodles yourself. That's easy and fun and you probably already have most of the ingredients in your pantry. There are recipes for fresh noodles throughout this book, but remember: When the recipe calls for fresh noodles, you can always make a big batch and freeze some for a quick weeknight meal or skip the noodle-making step and use your favorite store-bought fresh noodles.

We like to keep these noodles—or the ingredients for them—in our home pantry.

How does anyone know we've been eating pasta for 4,000 years? They found the leftovers! They dug up a bowl in China that still had long, thin noodles in it.

noodlecat

Bucatini
Bucatini is a dry, Italian pasta that looks like thick spaghetti with a long thin hole running through the middle of the noodle. The hole (*buco* in Italian) gives the pasta its name and allows it to cook more quickly than its wide diameter would suggest. The hot cooking water fills the hole and cooks the pasta from the inside out. One of the most famous dishes made with bucatini is the Roman favorite Bucatini all'Amatriciana. (See page 89.)

Cannelloni
Popular in Italy, where these "big reeds" were invented, Spain, England, and the United States, cannelloni are delicate sheets of fresh pasta—a lot like crepes—that are wrapped around a filling and baked. Team Sawyer likes to use kale and white beans topped with tomato sauce. (See page 51.) Bonus: Cannelloni is easy to prepare in advance.

Fregola
Fregola is a lot like couscous. It's made from semolina flour and water, worked into small spheres that are slightly larger than couscous, and then toasted, giving it a nuttier flavor. It's a staple in Sardinia, where it is usually boiled in a sauce, but I like to do something very untraditional with it. (See page 49.)

Fideo

Fideo is Spain's entry in the global noodle pantry. The thin, dried cylindrical noodles can resemble thin spaghetti or angel hair pasta, but the cooking style is very different. Traditionally, the dried pasta is broken into short 2-inch (5 cm) segments, toasted in olive oil and then cooked in a broth-y sauce. (See page 57.)

Macaroni

In Italy, they call it *maccheroncini*. The dried, tubular pasta was once so popular in Naples that the Neapolitans were nicknamed *mangiamaccheroni* ("macaroni eaters"). In the United States we know it best with a little bend: elbow macaroni. But we love to serve it the same way they used to on the streets of Naples, smothered in delicious cheese. (See page 46.)

Pierogi

Poland claims the pierogi, but you'll find versions of these stuffed dumplings throughout Eastern Europe. Half-moon-shaped pierogi are boiled and then baked or sautéed until golden brown and delicious, and they can be stuffed with anything from mashed potatoes to farmer's cheese to fresh fruit fillings to leftover pot roast. (Really, it's delicious. See page 33.)

Gnocchi

Gnocchi sound exotic, but they are just little fresh Italian dumplings made from egg, flour, and a third component, often potato or ricotta. Gnocchi are not named for famed Baroque composer Pietro Gnocchi; the name comes from *nocchio* ("knot of wood") or *noccho* ("knuckle"). Great gnocchi are frequently described as "pillowy" or "fluffy," and this light texture lets sauces shine. Team Sawyer likes them so much, there's a whole chapter dedicated to them. (See page 64.)

Orecchiette

Orecchiette look just like the name suggests: "little ears," with one thin edge, one thick edge, and a little bowl in the middle. This semolina pasta from the Puglia region of Italy is easy to find dried, but it is also easy to make fresh. The joke is all Italians from Puglia have big bent thumbs, from making all the orecchiette pasta. Either way, the little ears are best paired with a chunky, olive oil–based sauce. (See page 84.) All that goodness will get scooped up in the pasta.

Pizzoccheri

A pasta particular to the Trentino region of Italy, pizzoccheri are traditionally wide noodles made from the region's native buckwheat (though many versions also include semolina, which makes the pasta dough easier to work with). At our house, pizzoccheri is used to make a gratin so cheesy it's almost fondue. (See page 54.)

Potstickers

Asian potstickers, or gyoza, are probably the first of the stuffed pastas, dating all the way back to the Ming Dynasty. These thin-skinned dumplings are stuffed with meat, vegetables, and lots of flavor, and then steamed and sautéed until golden brown (until they almost *stick to the pot*). You can buy gyoza wrappers, but hot water dough is a flexible and useful recipe to learn. (See page 28.)

Ravioli

Probably the most popular of all stuffed pastas, ravioli is an Italian tradition, though exactly when and where in Italy it was invented is a topic of much debate. These typically square pastas can be stuffed with almost anything and are easy to shape, which means they are great for cooking with kids. (We throw ravioli parties! See page 38.)

Spaghetti

For so many people, *pasta* means "spaghetti," the long, cylindrical, semolina-based dried noodle extruded through a press. It was invented in Italy, of course, but is now eaten all over the world. (At our house, it's eaten with lobster. See page 83) Some estimate that spaghetti accounts for more than two-thirds of the world's pasta consumption.

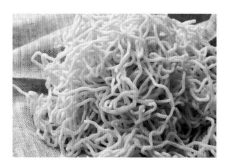

Ramen

Ramen noodles are a type of Japanese wheat noodle made with alkaline, which gives ramen its firm texture and yellow color. Ramen comes in all sorts of thicknesses and lengths and can be straight, wavy, or curly. Ramen noodles are, of course, an important ingredient in a bowl of ramen—but don't think of instant ramen!—and they are also used for saucy Mazeman Ramen (see page 90) and all kinds of other inventive recipes. (See chapters 7 and 9.)

Soba

In Japanese, *soba* means "buckwheat," or a long thin noodle made with buckwheat. Buckwheat is a great grain. It's healthier for you than all-purpose flours and it gives noodles a cool texture and toasty taste. You'll see soba served both hot and cold. (See page 131.)

Udon

These thick wheat noodles are a staple of Japanese cuisine. Udon is most often served in a broth. In Japan, the typical broth varies from region to region. (Try it with tofu. See page 94.) Udon can be served hot or cold.

Noodlecat in Morocco

The most famous pasta from Morocco doesn't really look like pasta at all. Couscous looks more like a little round grain of rice, but it's made from semolina flour, just like a lot of other noodles.

You can buy couscous in the store, but in some Moroccan homes, they still make couscous from scratch, the way people did hundreds and even thousands of years ago. It's a really fun project for the whole family. You get to use your hands a lot.

You start by spreading the flour out on a round tray and adding just a little bit of water. Then you make big circles with your hands, like you are playing with sand, rolling the flour into little balls. The pasta is sifted through screens so that it is all about the same size. The next step is to steam the couscous, then fluff it to separate the grains again. Finally, you let it dry. In some places in Morocco, you can see couscous drying in the sun.

When it's time to cook, there's a special pot called a *couscoussière* that you use to cook the pasta with meat and veggies. Yum!

How to Shop for Noodles

We love to take Catcher and Lulu shopping with us. It sparks all kinds of conversations about food and the kids feel like they have a say in planning dinner.

When we go shopping for noodles, we read the labels together. We're looking for minimal number of ingredients. There should be flour and water, alkaline when you are buying ramen, maybe some citric acid, but that's it. No enriched this or preserved that or bromated flour. I love it when I see a company tell you exactly what type of flour they use. You know they are serious about producing a good product.

We buy fresh, fresh-frozen, and dried pastas, in addition to what we make at home. The key is to shop at a store that sells a high volume of pasta, so you know that the package hasn't been sitting on the shelf for too long. You can get many types of pasta at your everyday grocery store, but it's worth exploring your local ethnic markets, too. You can find great pastas—and other cool ingredients—at many Asian and Eastern European markets.

Those are my only two tips: high-quality ingredients and a high-volume store. After that, it's trial and error. What tastes the best to you and your family? That's what you should be buying.

How to Cook Noodles

This whole book is about cooking noodles, of course, but there's two tips you'll see repeated throughout the book that will improve your pasta cooking immediately.

First, buy a large pasta pot with a strainer. You can lift the strainer right out of the pot when your pasta is finished cooking without dumping the precious cooking water. The cooking water is the secret ingredient in so many recipes. You can also use a large handheld strainer.

Then, when you fill the pasta pot with water, add salt. Lots of salt. The water should be so salty it tastes like the ocean. This will season your pasta and your sauce.

Everything Else

Of course, noodles aren't the only ingredient in your dinner, so it's also important to have a well-stocked pantry. There are some ingredients we are never without.

All-purpose organic flour
Cold-pressed, extra-virgin olive oil
Whole organic milk
Large organic eggs

You can tell I'm pretty particular about some of my ingredients, especially the ones I make pasta with. That comes from being a chef and from being a dad. There aren't a lot of ingredients in pasta—and I'm making that pasta for my kids—so I buy the best ingredients I can afford.

> **Add more salt. A lot of cooks don't realize how much salt pasta water needs.**
>
> *Chef Says*

Chapter 3

Stuffed

Almost every culture has a stuffed noodle recipe of some sort. Why? Besides the fact that they're delicious, they have always been an inexpensive, awesome way to feed a family. A little meat and a few vegetables can go a long way when your family is on a budget.

In Japan, it's crescent-shaped gyoza, with thin noodle skins traditionally wrapped around minced pork and cabbage. In China, slightly thicker noodles become purse-shaped wontons for boiling or deep-frying. In Poland, pierogi dough is made with potatoes and stuffed with any number of fillings from savory potato, cheese, and onions to sweet fruit jams. And of course, in Italy, there's ravioli, a Team Sawyer favorite.

Stuffed pastas are a great project for kids because you can stuff them with almost any ingredients you want and the stuffing process is pretty easy and fun. Stuffed noodles are forgiving: They taste good whether they're pretty or just pretty ugly.

Shumai Chicken

This is the gateway to stuffed pastas. It's easy to stuff and shape the purchased wonton skins into delicious little purses, and that will give you the confidence you need to tackle the slightly more complex stuffed pastas later in this chapter. The shape of these shumai is traditional, but the filling isn't. Usually you would stuff them with crab, mutton, or pork, but Team Sawyer votes for chicken.

INGREDIENTS

- 1 tablespoon (6 g) finely chopped ginger
- ¼ cup (25 g) finely chopped scallions
- 1 tablespoon (15 ml) soy sauce
- 1 teaspoon rice wine
- 1 teaspoon ground white pepper
- ½ teaspoon sugar
- 1 tablespoon (15 ml) oyster sauce
- Salt, to taste
- ¼ cup (31 g) sliced water chestnuts
- ¼ cup (25 g) sliced shiitake mushrooms
- 1 pound (454 g) ground chicken or duck, dark meat preferred
- 1 package (12 ounces, or 336 g) round wonton skins
- 1 to 2 tablespoons (15 to 30 ml) vegetable oil
- 1 cup (235 ml) water
- 1 recipe Crushed Peanut Dipping Sauce (recipe follows)

OTHER STUFF

Food processor
Plastic bag
Rubber band or kitchen string
Pastry brush
Nonstick pan with cover

HOW TO

1. In a food processor, combine the ginger, scallions, soy sauce, rice wine, white pepper, sugar, oyster sauce, and salt. Purée until smooth. Add the water chestnuts and shiitakes and pulse to purée, scraping the sides of the bowl occasionally to ensure an even texture. Add the ground chicken and pulse just to combine. Don't purée.

2. Place the filling mixture in the plastic bag and use the rubber band or string to force all the ingredients into one corner of the bag, for easy piping.

3. Brush the interior of a wonton wrapper lightly with water. Place the wonton in the center of your palm, wet side up, and fill with 2 tablespoons (30 g) filling. Push down on the filling to pack it tightly against the center of the wonton skin. Bring the edges of the wonton skin up the sides of the filling, making a purse. Crimp any overlapping wrapper at the top.

STOP (IF YOU WANT TO)! You can store stuffed, uncooked wontons in the freezer for up to 8 months until you are ready to cook them.

4. Warm the vegetable oil in a nonstick pan over medium-low heat. Place the shumai flat side down in the pan in concentric circles. The dumplings should not be touching each other. Now turn the heat up to medium-high and look for that golden brown color, about 3 to 5 minutes. Carefully add the water and cover immediately. Steam for 7 minutes, covered, then remove the cover and allow all the remaining liquid to evaporate and the bottoms to crisp. Serve with the dipping sauce.

YIELD: 6 appetizer servings

Noodlecat in China and Mongolia

If we could time travel back 300 years, we could eat the first shumai at a Mongolian teahouse—at breakfast! They created the yummy stuffed pasta as a snack to go with their morning tea. Three hundred years ago, it would have been weird to eat shumai at night, but now people in Mongolia and throughout China and Southeast Asia eat them all day long.

Because they're almost bite-size, shumai can make a good snack, or you can have several for a meal. You can select from many different kinds of shumai for breakfast, lunch, or dinner.

We don't know for sure what types of meat and vegetables the ancient Mongolians first stuffed into the dough to make shumai, but today people in the same region make them with ground mutton, ginger, and scallions. In Indonesia, shumai are stuffed with different types of fish. And in China, you can find shumai stuffed with pork and mushrooms, pumpkin or crab, depending on where you are and what season it is. What will you fill your shumai with?

Ginger-Pork Potstickers

Potstickers, or gyoza, are probably the first of the stuffed pastas, dating all the way back to the Ming Dynasty. The potsticker is a traditional food of the Chinese New Year celebration, but this version is a little more Japanese than Chinese and Team Sawyer likes to eat them any time. If your family goes crazy for them, too, consider picking up a simple plastic gyoza mold. It makes things much faster.

INGREDIENTS

- 3 tablespoons (45 ml) toasted sesame oil, divided
- 1 tablespoon (6 g) chopped ginger
- 4 cloves garlic, chopped
- ½ pound (227 g) 80% lean ground pork (Always be mindful of where your pork and shrimp are sourced from. Is it a local farm? Are the shrimp farm-raised?)
- ½ pound (227 g) shrimp, finely chopped
- ½ cup (45 g) chopped napa cabbage
- 2 tablespoons (12 g) chopped fermented bamboo
- 8 scallions, finely sliced
- 2 tablespoons (30 ml) charcoal-filtered soy sauce
- 2 limes, 1 zested and 1 cut into wedges
  Salt and pepper, to taste
- 1 recipe Hot Water Dough (recipe follows, page 30), or 2 packages (12 ounces, or 336 g) gyoza wrappers
  All-purpose flour, as needed
- 1 cup (235 ml) water
- 1 recipe Dipping Sauce, J Style (recipe follows, page 30)

OTHER STUFF

Food processor
Plastic bag
Rubber band or kitchen string
Rolling pin
2-inch (5 cm) ring mold
Parchment paper
Pastry brush
Nonstick pan with cover
Large serving plate

HOW TO

1. In the food processor, combine 2 tablespoons (30 ml) sesame oil, ginger, and garlic and process until smooth. Add the pork and shrimp and pulse to purée the ingredients, scraping the sides of the bowl to ensure an even texture. Add the cabbage, bamboo, scallions, soy sauce, and lime zest and pulse just to combine. Don't purée. Add salt and pepper to taste.

2. Place the mixture in the plastic bag and use the rubber band or string to force all the ingredients into one corner of the bag, for easy piping.

3. If you are working with packaged gyoza wrappers, skip to step 4. Otherwise, dust your work station with flour and divide the dough in half. Using a rolling pin, roll the dough to a ½-inch (1.3 cm) thickness. Using the ring mold, cut out 2-inch (5 cm) circles. Roll each circle until ¼-inch (6 mm) thick. Store the rounds on parchment paper. Repeat with the remaining dough.

4. Brush the inside of each dough round or packaged gyoza wrapper with water lightly but completely. Add 1 tablespoon (15 g) filling in the center of each round. Gently fold the dough over the filling and crimp the dumpling edges to achieve a proper seal and the classic gyoza look. (Check out the picture!)

5. Warm the remaining 1 tablespoon (15 ml) sesame oil in a nonstick pan over medium-low heat. Place the potstickers flat side down in the pan in concentric circles. The dumplings should be overlapping slightly at the corners. Now turn the heat up to medium-high and look for that golden brown color, about 3 to 5 minutes. Carefully add the water and cover immediately. Steam for 7 minutes, covered, then remove the cover and allow all the remaining liquid to evaporate and the bottoms to crisp.

6. For a beautiful presentation, remove the pan from the heat, invert a large plate over the pan and turn it all over like a pineapple upside-down cake. Serve with the lime wedges and dipping sauce.

YIELD: 4 appetizer servings

Hot Water Dough

It's easy enough to buy potsticker (or gyoza) wrappers, but it can be fun to make the dough yourself. Bonus: You can use this same technique to make gluten-free potsticker dough. Replace the all-purpose flour with 2½ cups (313 g) rice flour and 1½ cups (188 g) tapioca flour.

INGREDIENTS
1½ cups (355 ml) water
 1 teaspoon vegetable oil
 4 cups (500 g) all-purpose flour
 ½ teaspoon kosher salt

OTHER STUFF
Small saucepan
Stand mixer with dough hook attachment
Plastic wrap
Dish towel

HOW TO
1. Combine the water and oil in the saucepan and bring to a simmer over low heat.

2. In the stand mixer with the dough hook attachment, combine the flour and salt. Slowly add the simmering water to the flour in ¼-cup (60 ml) increments while mixing at medium speed. Continue mixing for 10 minutes.

3. Remove the dough from the stand mixer. Wrap in plastic wrap and cover with a damp kitchen towel.

WAIT! Allow the dough to rest at room temperature for at least 1 hour.

YIELD: 3½ pounds (1.6 kg)

Dipping Sauce, J Style

This is a big, tangy punch of umami, that fifth basic flavor that can be translated as "deliciousness." You can change up this Japanese-style sauce to match your own sense of deliciousness with fish sauce, miso, or wasabi.

INGREDIENTS
 1 teaspoon Asian chili sauce
 ½ cup (120 ml) soy sauce
 2 teaspoons toasted sesame oil
 ½ teaspoon sugar
 1 tablespoon (15 ml) rice wine vinegar
 1 tablespoon (6 g) finely sliced scallion
 1 teaspoon finely grated fresh ginger

OTHER STUFF
Bowl

HOW TO
In the bowl combine all the ingredients and serve at room temperature.

YIELD: ¾ cup (180 ml)

Crushed Peanut Dipping Sauce

This dipping sauce is slightly spicy, so if you don't have a family of fire breathers, just omit the chiles. This sauce is also great with miso, so if you love that flavor, add some.

INGREDIENTS

½ cup (130 g) smooth natural peanut butter or sunflower seed butter

¼ cup (60 ml) soy sauce

2 tablespoons (30 ml) spicy Szechuan oil

2 tablespoons (30 ml) sesame oil

¼ cup (24 g) sliced Chinese black garlic

2 cloves garlic, smashed

3 tablespoons (24 g) grated fresh ginger

1 tablespoon (15 ml) sambal oelek or another Asian chili sauce

1 tablespoon (20 g) honey

2 limes, zested and juiced

½ cup (120 ml) water

1 tablespoon (6 g) ground black pepper

½ cup (75 g) crushed, roasted, salted peanuts

Salt, to taste

OTHER STUFF

Food processor

HOW TO

Combine all the ingredients in the food processor and process until smooth.

YIELD: 1½ cups (355 ml)

WEAR GLOVES
Chef has a rule: Whenever you are working with raw meat, you have to wear gloves and use a cutting board and a knife meant just for the meat. You don't want the meat to touch anything else. When you are done working with the meat, you put the cutting board and the knife in the dishwasher and throw away your gloves.

noodlecat

Farmer's Cheese and Pot Roast Pierogi

Almost every European culture has a version of the pierogi and their own spelling for this dumpling. We always make a big batch of pierogi. People love them no matter how you spell the name. You can also combine all scraps of dough during the pierogi-making process and save it. This dough will not be stuffed but is a nice chewy Ukrainian varenecky variation to be enjoyed just blanched and sauced like a potato gnocchi.

INGREDIENTS

2 large organic eggs, divided

1 cup (230 g) sour cream, divided

6 tablespoons (84 g) salted butter, divided

¼ cup (60 ml) vegetable oil

2 tablespoons (8 g) fresh herbs, divided (choose your favorite: chives, scallions, parsley)

   Salt and pepper, to taste

2 cups (250 g) all-purpose flour, plus extra for rolling

1 tablespoon (15 ml) water

1 recipe Farmer's Cheese Pierogi Filling (recipe follows) or Pot Roast Pierogi Filling (recipe follows)

¼ cup (60 ml) leftover pot roast liquid or pasta water (for Pot Roast Pierogi Filling)

¼ lemon, zested and juiced

OTHER STUFF

Stand mixer or large bowl

Plastic wrap

Rolling pin

2 to 3-inch (5 to 7.5 cm) ring mold

Parchment paper

Small bowl

Pastry brush

Pasta pot with strainer

Medium saucepan

Perogi, pyrogy, perogie, perogy, pirohi— The word comes from the Polish word for *canoe.* That's what pierogi look like.

noodlecat

HOW TO

1. In a stand mixer or large bowl, combine 1 of the eggs, ¾ cup (173 g) of the sour cream, ¼ cup (56 g) of the butter, the oil, 1 tablespoon (4 g) of the herbs, and salt to taste. Mix for 3 minutes to combine. Add the flour in three parts, mixing between each addition.

WAIT! Cover the dough in plastic wrap and refrigerate for at least 1 hour or up to 3 days.

2. When ready to make the pierogi, dust the counter with flour and split the dough in half. Roll half the dough until it is ¹⁄₁₆-inch (1.5 mm) thick. Using a ring mold, cut the dough into circles. Stack the rounds with parchment paper between them. Repeat with the remaining dough.

3. Prepare an egg wash by beating the remaining egg lightly with the water in a small bowl with a fork. Brush the inside of each round with the egg wash. Place 1 tablespoon (15 g) pierogi filling in the center of the round and fold the dough over it into a half-moon shape. Crimp the edges with a fork to seal.

WAIT (IF YOU WANT TO)! You can store these pierogi in the refrigerator or freeze for up to 4 months until you are ready to cook. Don't stack the fresh pierogi. They are sticky.

4. Fill a large pot with water and season with salt until it tastes like seawater. Bring to a boil over high heat. Reduce to a simmer and cook the pierogi for 5 minutes. Transfer the pierogi to a saucepan with some water still clinging to the noodles, flat side down. Reserve ¼ cup (60 ml) pasta water, if using the Farmer's Cheese Pierogi Filling.

5. Place the saucepan over medium-high heat. Add 1 tablespoon (14 g) of the butter and cook until the water evaporates and the pierogi are golden brown and delicious, about 1 minute on each side. Add the reserved pasta water or the pot roast liquid, the remaining 1 tablespoon (4 g) herbs, and the remaining 1 tablespoon (14 g) butter. Reduce the heat to medium-low and simmer, stirring gently, until a smooth, creamy sauce forms, about 3 minutes. Garnish with the remaining ¼ cup (58 g) sour cream.

YIELD: 4 appetizer servings

You can also use a special dough press to mold your pierogi. Place the dough round on the press.

Place the filling in the center of the dough.

Close the mold to firmly crimp the edges.

Noodlecat in Poland

In Poland, you can eat pierogi for both dinner and dessert. These noodles can be stuffed with almost anything. Some of the most popular choices are meat and onion or fresh strawberries. Guess which one is for dessert.

Pierogi aren't the only noodles in Poland. You might also eat *kopytka* (a lot like gnocchi) and *kluski* (dumplings). But pierogi are definitely the country's best-known noodle. You'll see them everywhere at Christmastime. They are part of the traditional Polish Christmas Eve dinner. Those ones are filled with mushrooms and sauerkraut.

Everyone loves pierogi. In Alberta, Canada, there's a 25-foot (7.6 m) tall sculpture of a pierogi on a fork. In Niagara Falls, New York, a chef cooked an enormous pierogi. It was more than 170 pounds (77 kg), filled with lots and lots of potatoes and cheese and topped with onions. And back in Poland, someone set a world record for pierogi making: 1,663 pierogi in 100 minutes. How fast can you make them?

Farmer's Cheese Pierogi Filling

Catcher and Lulu don't like onions, except in onion soup, but Amelia and I love onions. Our trick: Instead of garnishing a dish with onions, we put them inside whenever possible. It's not really hiding the onion. It's just letting them be backstage as opposed to front and center.

INGREDIENTS

2   tablespoons (28 g) salted butter

½   cup (80 g) diced white onion

2   cups (460 g) farmer's cheese (choose your favorite: strained cottage cheese, goat cheese, chopped Brie)

1   cup (225 g) leftover mashed potatoes

1   tablespoon (4 g) fresh herbs (choose your favorite: chives, scallions, parsley)

Salt and pepper, to taste

OTHER STUFF

Sauté pan

Large bowl

Plastic bag

Rubber band or kitchen string

HOW TO

1. In a sauté pan over low heat, melt the butter and add the onion, cooking until soft, about 30 to 45 minutes.

2. In the large bowl, combine the sautéed onions, cheese, potatoes, and herbs. Season to taste with salt and pepper. Place the mixture in the plastic bag and use the rubber band or sting to force all the ingredients into one corner of the bag, for easy piping.

YIELD: 3 cups (705 g)

> **HOW NOT TO MAKE PIEROGI**
> Chef tells a story about his friend's grandmother who said that to make the best pierogi you squish the filled pierogi in your armpit and nibble around the edges. He's only kidding! That's not how you make pierogi.

noodlecat

Pot Roast Pierogi Filling

This is a great use for leftover pot roast, or really any meaty leftover. In our house, we make this pierogi filling from sauerbraten, osso buco, meatloaf, pork chops, or whatever we have.

INGREDIENTS

 2 tablespoons (28 g) salted butter
½ cup (80 g) diced white onion
 2 cups (450 g) shredded pot roast meat
½ cup (50 g) shredded hard cheese (choose your favorite: Parmesan, dry Jack)
 1 tablespoon (4 g) fresh herbs (choose your favorite: chive, scallion, parsley)
    Salt and pepper, to taste

OTHER STUFF

Sauté pan
Large bowl
Plastic bag
Rubber band or kitchen string

HOW TO

1. In a sauté pan over low heat, melt the butter and add the onion, cooking until soft, about 30 to 45 minutes.

2. In the large bowl, combine the sautéed onions, meat, cheese and herbs. Season to taste with salt and pepper. Place the mixture in the plastic bag and use the rubber band or sting to force all the ingredients into one corner of the bag, for easy piping.

YIELD: 2½ pounds (1.1 kg)

> Okay. NoodleCat is right. That's not how you make pierogi. But, they are easy to make using a rolling pin, a fork (or your fingers!), or a special mold made just for pierogi time.

Chef Says

How to Throw a Ravioli Party

Our family is big on the ravioli party. It turns our usual family dinner into a fun afternoon activity. It's really a four-step process. Step 1: roll the fresh pasta dough; step 2: pick the filling; step 3: shape the ravioli; step 4: cook it; and step 5: Eat! There are lots of projects here that the kids can help with, but their favorite parts are always step 3 (shaping) and step 5 (eating). This recipe feeds our family of four. You can make an additional batch of dough and double the filling if you want a bigger ravioli party or some pasta to freeze for another meal.

1 Roll the Fresh Pasta Dough

If you don't have or don't want to use a stand mixer and pasta machine, you can knead and roll the ravioli dough by hand. It takes some time, but it's also a lot of fun to play with your food that way.

INGREDIENTS
- 5 large organic eggs
- 5 teaspoons (25 ml) water, at room temperature
- 5 teaspoons (25 ml) cold-pressed, extra-virgin oil
- 4 cups (500 g) organic all-purpose flour, plus more as needed

OTHER STUFF
Stand mixer with a dough hook or large bowl
Plastic wrap
Pasta machine or rolling pin
Parchment paper
Dish towel

HOW TO

1. In the bowl of the stand mixer or in a big bowl, combine the eggs, water, and olive oil and mix well. Add the flour in four parts, mixing well after each addition. Mix or knead the dough until it forms an elastic, pliable ball, about 15 minutes. If the dough is wet and sticky, you can add more flour as needed. (But you can't add more liquid if it's too dry, so we always err on the side of wet dough.) The amount of flour you need may vary. Dough can behave differently depending on the weather.

WAIT! Allow the dough to rest, covered in plastic wrap, in the refrigerator for at least 30 minutes or up to 48 hours. This step is super important because it allows the wet and dry molecules of the dough to come into contact with one another and allows the dough to become completely hydrated.

2. Divide the dough into four batches. Set the pasta machine on the thickest noodle setting and feed one batch of dough through the machine. Reduce the noodle setting and feed the dough through again. Repeat until you reach the second thinnest setting. When you are done, you will have a sheet of dough about 18-inches (45.7 cm) long. Repeat with the three remaining batches of dough. (If you are working with a rolling pin, dust the counter with flour and roll each batch of dough until you have a sheet less than ¼-inch [6 mm] thick.)

3. For ravioli, cut the dough into 3-inch (7.5 cm) square pieces and dust each one with flour. If you are using the dough for Lasagna (page 58) or Tuscan Kale and White Bean Cannelloni (page 51), cut into pieces 4-inches (10 cm) long by 2-inches (5 cm) wide. Store them stacked with a piece of parchment between each piece, covered with plastic wrap and a dish towel, in the refrigerator for up to 1 week.

YIELD: 15 ounces (420 g)

> The thinnest setting on the pasta machine is for angel hair pasta and for the professional only. If you are having trouble working with the dough, the third thinnest setting will make good ravioli, too. It will get easier to go thinner once you have had more practice.
>
> *Chef Says*

2 Pick the Filling

One of the best things about ravioli—and any stuffed pasta—is that you can change it up. You can make a great ravioli filling from almost anything the kids pick out at the farmers' market. These are some of Team Sawyer's seasonal favorites.

Spring Minty Pea Ravioli Filling

INGREDIENTS

- 1   cup fresh (145 g) or fresh-frozen (134 g) sweet peas
- ½   cup (123 g) ricotta cheese or fromage blanc
- ¼   cup (25 g) grated Parmesan cheese
- ½   tablespoon (1 g) chopped mint
- ½   tablespoon (2 g) chopped parsley
- 1   lemon, zested and juiced
- 1   tablespoon (15 ml) cold-pressed, extra-virgin olive oil
  Salt and pepper, to taste

OTHER STUFF

Food processor (or large bowl)
Large plastic freezer bag or pastry bag
Rubber band or kitchen string

HOW TO

1. Purée all the ingredients (except a small handful of peas, which you'll use as a garnish) in the food processor, tasting to make sure you like the seasoning. If you are working with a knife instead of a food processor, dice the peas and herbs finely, and then mix vigorously in the bowl.

2. Place the purée in the plastic bag and use the rubber band or string to force all the ingredients into one corner of the bag, for easy piping.

YIELD: 3 cups (705 g)

Summer Roasted Cauliflower and Potato Ravioli Filling

INGREDIENTS

- ½   head cauliflower, chopped
- 2   small waxy potatoes
- 1   tablespoon (15 ml) cold-pressed, extra-virgin olive oil
  Salt and pepper, to taste
- 1   cup (113 g) grated dry Jack cheese
- ½   cup (56 g) grated fresh mozzarella cheese

OTHER STUFF

Small baking dish
Food mill or food processor
Large plastic freezer bag or pastry bag
Rubber band or kitchen string

HOW TO

1. Preheat the oven to 350°F (180°C, or gas mark 4). Coat the cauliflower and potatoes in olive oil and sprinkle with salt and pepper to taste. Place the vegetables in the baking dish and roast until fully cooked, about 40 minutes.

2. Peel the potatoes and reserve a few cauliflower florets for garnish. While the vegetables are still warm, purée the potatoes and cauliflower in a food mill or food processor. Allow the mixture to cool and fold in the cheeses. Taste for seasoning.

3. Place the purée in the plastic bag and use the rubber band or string to force all the ingredients into one corner of the bag, for easy piping.

YIELD: 3 cups (705 g)

Fall Sweet Italian Sausage and Peppers

INGREDIENTS

½ cup (44 g) diced fennel
½ cup (74 g) diced red pepper
2 cloves garlic, minced
1 teaspoon cold-pressed, extra-virgin olive oil
1 pound (454 g) sweet Italian sausage, casing removed
½ cup (50 g) grated Parmesan cheese
Salt and pepper, to taste

OTHER STUFF

Sauté pan
Potato masher (optional)
Large plastic freezer bag or pastry bag
Rubber band or kitchen string

HOW TO

1. In a sauté pan over medium heat, sauté the fennel, pepper, and garlic in the olive oil until cooked through. Add the sausage and cook for another 10 minutes, stirring frequently to keep the texture fine and the mixture homogenous. (Hint: A potato masher is great for that.) Allow the filling to cool, still stirring or mashing occasionally, and then add the Parmesan cheese. Season with salt and pepper to taste.

2. Place the filling in the plastic bag and use the rubber band or string to force all the ingredients into one corner of the bag, for easy piping.

YIELD: 3 cups (705 g)

Winter Butternut Squash and Brown Butter

INGREDIENTS

1 tablespoon (14 g) salted butter
1 cup (140 g) peeled and diced winter squash
Salt and pepper, to taste
6 leaves sage, minced
1 orange, zested
Pinch of nutmeg
½ cup (124 g) mascarpone cheese
1 tablespoon (5 g) grated Parmesan cheese

OTHER STUFF

Ovenproof sauté pan
Food mill or food processor
Large plastic freezer bag or pastry bag
Rubber band or kitchen string

HOW TO

1. Preheat the oven to 350°F (180°C, or gas mark 4).

2. In the sauté pan over medium heat, cook the butter until it is lightly browned and smells like toasted nuts, about 5 minutes. Add the squash to the pan, season with salt and pepper, and cook for an additional 5 minutes. Add the sage and roast the mixture in the oven until cooked through, about 20 minutes.

3. Purée the warm squash mixture in a food mill or food processor. Fold in the orange zest (reserving a little to garnish the ravioli), nutmeg, and mascarpone. Allow the filling to cool, stirring occasionally, and add the Parmesan cheese.

4. Place the filling in the plastic bag and use the rubber band or string to force all the ingredients into one corner of the bag, for easy piping.

YIELD: 2 cups (470 g)

3 Shape the Ravioli

This is the really fun part. Set up a simple assembly line and everyone can make their own ravioli. It's a quick project without a lot of rules (Don't throw ravioli at your sister!) and ravioli tastes good in any shape or size.

INGREDIENTS

1   recipe precut ravioli dough (see step 1, page 39) or
    1 pound (454 g) purchased fresh or frozen pasta sheets
1   large egg, beaten with 1 tablespoon (15 ml) water
2   cups (470 g) ravioli filling in a plastic bag for piping
    (see step 2, page 40)
    Organic all-purpose flour, as needed

OTHER STUFF

A small tray for each ravioli maker
Pastry brush
Fluted pastry wheel or knife
Cookie sheet
A small tray for each ravioli maker

HOW TO

1. Set up an assembly line on your kitchen table and give each ravioli maker a small tray to work on as he or she moves through the stations.

   Station 1: Precut ravioli dough
   Station 2: Egg wash
   Station 3: Ravioli filling in a plastic bag for piping
   Station 4: Fluted pastry wheel and/or knife
   Station 5: Cookie sheet dusted with flour for storage

Place a piece of dough on a tray.

Brush the edges with egg wash.

Pipe 1 tablespoon (15 g) of filling in the center.

Trim the edges of the ravioli.

Fold the dough over the filling and seal the edges.

Place the finished ravioli on the cookie sheet.

2. Demonstrate how to make ravioli. First, dust your work tray with a little flour. At station one, put one piece of ravioli dough on the tray. At the second station, brush the edges of the dough lightly with egg wash. At station three, pipe 1 tablespoon (15 g) of filling in the center of the dough. Fold the dough over the filling into a triangle or a rectangular shape and press the edges to seal. At station four, trim the edges of the ravioli with a fluted pastry wheel or knife. At station five, place the finished ravioli on a cookie sheet. You can freeze these for up to 4 months until you are ready to cook.

3. Let everyone help. The great thing about ravioli: It's okay if they are different shapes and sizes. If you want to make an extra big one by sandwiching the filling between two sheets of dough, that's delicious. Keep making ravioli until the filling or the dough runs out. (It rarely happens at exactly the same time.)

YIELD: 60 to 70 ravioli

Have you ever made ravioli before? Me neither. But Chef says it is as easy as making a peanut butter and jelly sandwich. I guess the dough is like the bread and the filling is like the peanut butter and jelly. You want just the right amount of peanut butter and jelly so it doesn't squish out everywhere.

noodlecat

4 Cook It

Time to get your homemade ravioli on the dinner table. Ravioli only take a few minutes to cook. The kids can set the dinner table in the meantime.

INGREDIENTS

    Homemade ravioli (see step 3, page 42)
¼   cup (56 g) salted butter, divided
4   tablespoons (8 g) fresh herbs, divided (choose your
    favorite: parsley, basil, mint, oregano)
½   cup (50 g) grated Parmesan cheese, divided
    Juice from 1 orange (for winter filling only)
2   tablespoons (12 g) toasted bread crumbs

OTHER STUFF
Pasta pot with strainer
Small saucepan
Serving plate

HOW TO

1. Fill a large pot with water and season with salt until it tastes like seawater. Bring to a boil over high heat. Reduce to a simmer. Cook 5 ravioli at a time, simmering for about 5 minutes.

2. Transfer the 5 ravioli to the saucepan with some pasta water still on the noodles. The small addition of some of the pasta water allows all the sauce ingredients to emulsify together and form a more cohesive sauce. Add 1 tablespoon (14 g) of the butter, 1 teaspoon of the herbs, 1 tablespoon (5 g) of the Parmesan cheese, and the orange juice if using the winter filling. Simmer over medium-low heat, stirring gently, until a smooth and creamy sauce forms, about 3 minutes. Transfer to a plate. Repeat with the remaining ravioli.

3. Garnish each dish with ½ tablespoon (3 g) bread crumbs, 1 tablespoon (5 g) of the remaining Parmesan, a sprinkling of herbs, and any additional garnish you might like.

YIELD: 4 servings

Chapter 4

Baked

I'll bake almost anything. It's my go-to cooking technique at home. It's great because when there's something in the oven, you're cooking but you also have some free time to do other things around the kitchen and spend some time with the kids. Plus, you don't have to worry about little hands reaching for the handle of a saucepan on the stove top.

I like to prepare a dish such as Team Sawyer's favorite Cheesy Broccoli and Macaroni Bake-Up before the kids get home from school. When they walk in the house, they can smell it. There's something satisfying about the smell of something baking. While dinner is cooking, Catcher and Lulu can help me cut vegetables or make a salad. If we're making a baked pasta on the weekend, they like to help mix the cheese into quick dishes such as Pizzoccheri Gratin (ooey-gooey cheese is the secret in almost every baked pasta dish) and layer all the ingredients in the lasagna.

Macaroni Casserole (a.k.a. Cheesy Broccoli and Macaroni Bake-Up)

We call this a "bake-up" because Amelia doesn't like the word "casserole." Whatever you call it, you'll love this mac 'n' cheese. You never have to feel guilty about eating it, because we use broth rather than cream and add broccoli because it tastes great. And it's easy for a weeknight meal. You can make a huge batch of the cheese sauce and freeze it. Every time you want mac 'n' cheese, all you have to do is boil the noodles, add the sauce, and bake.

INGREDIENTS

- 1 cup (235 ml) chicken or vegetable stock or water
- 2 cups (473 ml) organic whole milk
- ½ cup (63 g) organic all-purpose flour
- 1 tablespoon (14 g) salted butter, at room temperature
- 3 cups (240 g) grated sharp cheddar cheese
- ½ cup (124 g) ricotta cheese
- ¼ cup (25 g) grated Parmesan cheese, divided
- 1 pound (454 g) elbow macaroni
- 1 head broccoli, cut into florets with stems peeled and sliced
- 2 tablespoons (13 g) toasted bread crumbs
- 2 tablespoons (30 ml) cold-pressed, extra-virgin olive oil

OTHER STUFF

- 9-inch (23 cm) square baking dish
- Medium saucepan
- Large bowl
- Whisk
- Pasta pot with strainer
- Aluminum foil

HOW TO

1. Preheat the oven to 400°F (200°C, or gas mark 6). Lightly oil the baking dish.

2. Combine the stock and milk in a medium saucepan and bring to a boil over medium-high heat. In a separate bowl, combine the flour, butter, cheddar, ricotta, and 2 tablespoons (12 g) of the Parmesan cheese and mix vigorously. Slowly whisk the cheese mixture into the milk mixture. Reduce the heat to medium and simmer until slightly thickened, about 10 minutes, stirring often. Remove from the heat.

STOP (IF YOU WANT TO)! You can freeze this cheese sauce for up to 2 months for a quick dinner later in the week. This sauce is so versatile and works well with tuna, turkey, or tofu, whatever you feel like! But for now, let's keep going for dinner tonight.

3. Fill the pasta pot with water and season with salt until it tastes like seawater. Bring to a boil over high heat. Add the macaroni and cook until al dente, about 6 minutes. Add the broccoli and cook for 1 minute. Remove from the heat and drain.

4. In a large bowl, combine the cheese sauce and noodles with the broccoli florets and stems.

5. Transfer the noodle mixture to the dish. Top with the bread crumbs and the remaining 2 tablespoons (12 g) Parmesan and drizzle with the oil. Cover with aluminum foil and bake for 20 minutes. Remove the foil and continue baking until lightly browned and crisp on top, about 6 minutes.

YIELD: 4 to 6 servings

Freaky Fast-Baked Fregola

This is a nontraditional approach to cooking fregola, which is a cousin of couscous. Here, I use carrots, but you can replace them with almost anything. I like to add asparagus or chickpeas (I add beans to everything we cook at home) and Catcher and Lulu often ask for sausage. They are meat maniacs and will eat anything with sausage. There's really no wrong answer to the question, "What goes with fregola?" It's the chef's choice.

INGREDIENTS
- 2 cups (316 g) fregola
- ½ cup (65 g) diced carrot
- 6 tablespoons (36 g) grated Parmesan cheese, divided
- 3 cups (705 ml) water
- 2 tablespoons (28 g) salted butter
- 1 bunch fresh herbs, tied with kitchen string (choose your favorite: rosemary, sage, thyme, bay)
- ¼ cup (38 g) grated fresh mozzarella
- 2 tablespoons (14 g) toasted bread crumbs
- 1 tablespoon (15 ml) cold-pressed, extra-virgin olive oil

OTHER STUFF
- 9 x 13-inch (23 x 33 cm) baking dish
- Large bowl
- Aluminum foil

HOW TO
1. Preheat the oven to 400°F (200°C, or gas mark 6). Grease the baking dish.

2. In the large bowl, combine the fregola, carrot, 2 tablespoons (12 g) of the Parmesan, and the water. Transfer the mixture to the baking dish and top with the butter and add herbs. Cover with aluminum foil and bake for 15 minutes. Uncover the pan, top with the mozzarella, bread crumbs, and 2 tablespoons (12 g) of the Parmesan. Bake an additional 15 minutes, until golden brown and delicious. Remove the herbs, drizzle with the olive oil and the remaining 2 tablespoons (12 g) Parmesan.

YIELD: 4 appetizer servings

FREGOLA IS FUN
You don't have to, but you can make fregola at home. It's pretty fun. All you need is a big bowl of semolina. Sprinkle in a little water with your fingertips until little clumps form. Then all you have to do is dry them out in the oven.

noodlecat

Tuscan Kale and White Bean Cannelloni

Traditionally, cannelloni are filled with cheese, cheese, and more cheese. For me, though, whenever I see a recipe like that I always want to figure out how to get some vegetables into the dish. Kale and white beans are a classic Tuscan combination, so I added those to the filling to make it more balanced. Don't worry—there's still milk and cream and cheese in there, too.

Cannelloni (or manicotti) is very popular in Spain, as it was imported by Italian bricklayers in the nineteenth century. It is seen as a celebratory dish with a decent amount of advance prep, followed by an easy execution. It's commonly made for St. Stephen's Day on December 26 and filled with the treats of Christmas, such as capon or roast goose. Cannelloni is also affectionately referred to as "big reeds" in Italian.

INGREDIENTS

- 1 recipe Fresh Pasta Dough (page 39), rolled and cut into 4 x 2-inch (10 x 5 cm) pieces
- 1 tablespoon (15 ml) cold-pressed, extra-virgin olive oil, plus more for drizzling
- 1 shallot, finely diced
- 2 head garlic, peeled and smashed
  Salt and pepper, to taste
- 3 cups (210 g) chopped kale, thick stems removed
  Pinch of all-purpose flour
- 2 cups (470 ml) whole milk
- 1 cup (235 ml) cream
- 1 cup (250 g) cooked white beans
- ¾ cup (75 g) grated Parmesan cheese, divided
- 2 cups (475 ml) Basic Tomato Sauce (recipe follows), or your favorite tomato sauce
- ½ cup (55 g) grated provolone picante

OTHER STUFF

Pasta pot with strainer
Large bowl filled with ice and water
Parchment paper
Large sauté pan
9 x 13-inch (23 x 33 cm) baking dish

HOW TO

1. Fill the large pot with water and season with salt until it tastes like seawater. Bring to a boil over high heat. Working in batches of four or five, cook the pasta sheets for 5 minutes, until softened but not cooked through. Transfer the blanched pasta sheets to a large bowl of ice and water to cool completely. Reserve ½ cup (120 ml) of the pasta water. Drain the cooled noodles, drizzle lightly with olive oil and toss to coat, and layer between parchment paper.

STOP (IF YOU WANT TO)! You can store the blanched pasta sheets in the refrigerator until dinner or freeze them for up to 4 months for later use.

2. Heat the 1 tablespoon (15 ml) olive oil in a large sauté pan over medium-high heat. Add the shallot and garlic, season with salt and pepper, and cook until translucent but not browned, about 4 minutes. Add the kale and a splash of pasta water, season again with salt and pepper, and cook until partially wilted, about 3 minutes. Add the flour, stir, and then add the milk and cream. Stirring constantly, bring the mixture to a boil and cook until reduced by half. Remove the pan from the heat and stir in the white beans and ½ cup (50 g) of the Parmesan. Cool to room temperature. The mixture should be just thick enough to scoop.

Chef Says

3. Preheat the oven to 350°F (180°C, or gas mark 4) and oil the baking dish.

4. To assemble the cannelloni rolls, spread 3 tablespoons (45 g) of the kale mixture on each pasta sheet. Roll each pasta sheet into a short cylinder. Place the filled cannelloni, seam down, into the baking dish touching the one beside it. Cover the cannelloni with the tomato sauce and top with the provolone and remaining ¼ cup (25 g) Parmesan. Bake for 40 minutes, or until golden brown and bubbly.

Yield: 8 servings

Basic Tomato Sauce

At home, we never, ever, ever buy canned tomato sauce. This smooth, basic tomato sauce is just so easy and tasty. You can make it with fresh or canned tomatoes and you can use it in lots of different ways.

INGREDIENTS

- 1 Vidalia onion, chopped
- 1 carrot, chopped
- 1 stalk celery, chopped
- 2 cloves garlic
- 1 teaspoon dried oregano
- 2 tablespoons (30 ml) cold-pressed, extra-virgin olive oil
   Salt and pepper, to taste
- 4 cups (900 g) chopped canned tomatoes or 6 cups (1080 g) chopped fresh tomatoes
- ½ bunch basil, tied with kitchen string

OTHER STUFF

   Food processor
   Large saucepan with cover
   Kitchen string

HOW TO

1. In a food processor, combine the onion, carrot, celery, garlic, oregano, and olive oil. Process to your preferred consistency.

2. Transfer the vegetable mixture to the saucepan, season with salt and pepper, cover, and cook over medium heat for 15 minutes, stirring occasionally. Add the tomatoes and cook for an additional 15 minutes. Remove from the heat and add a tied bunch of basil. The basil flavor will steep while the sauce cools. Remove the basil before using.

YIELD: 1 quart (940 ml)

Noodlecat in Spain

When you think about places with a long tradition of pasta, you don't always think of Spain, but you should: People say that the Spanish first brought noodles to the United States!

In Spain—particularly in Barcelona—you can find *fideo, canelones,* and *galets.* The word *fideo* means "noodle" in Spanish, but when people ask for fideo they usually mean a thin noodle like angel hair. It's often broken into short pieces in soups or cooked like rice in a paella. (There's a recipe for that in this book.) *Canelones* are hollow tubes meant for stuffing, just like the Italian cannelloni. And *galets* are big snail shell–shaped pasta.

Galets are eaten on Christmas Eve or Christmas Day in a soup called *escudella a Nadal.* The soup simmers all day with all sorts of different vegetables and meats, including one really big meatball called a *pilota.* The pasta is served with the broth, and all the vegetables and meats are served later. *Galets* are so Christmas that the city of Barcelona decorates the streets with giant plastic *galet* sculptures that light up at night.

Pizzoccheri Gratin

This is a classic from Trentino, the beautiful mountainous region in Italy where Amelia's family is from. This dish is soul-satisfying comfort food, based on pantry staples such as cheese, potatoes, and pasta. The cheese choice is entirely yours. We love using fontina, but Taleggio, Brie, buffalo mozzarella, or any stretchy, ooey gooey cheese is great, too.

INGREDIENTS

½   cup (112 g) salted butter

½   teaspoon toasted caraway seeds, cracked

½   teaspoon poppy seeds, cracked

3   or 4 sprigs of sage

1   russet potato, peeled and diced

1   pound (454 g) large, flat buckwheat noodles or whole wheat noodles

½   head napa cabbage, shredded

1   cup (110 g) grated fontina cheese, divided

1   cup (100 g) grated Parmesan cheese, divided

    Salt and pepper, to taste

    Oil

½   cup (120 ml) vegetable broth

1   cup (115 g) toasted bread crumbs

2   tablespoons (8 g) chopped parsley

OTHER STUFF

Medium saucepan

Large saucepan

Large bowl

9 x 13-inch (23 x 33 cm) baking dish or oven-safe pan

HOW TO

1. Preheat the oven to 350°F (180°C, or gas mark 4).

2. In a medium saucepan over low heat, melt the butter. Add the caraway seeds, poppy seeds, and sage. Sauté until the butter is nut brown, 15 to 20 seconds.

3. Bring a large saucepan of water to a boil. Add the potatoes and cook for 7 minutes. Remove the potatoes. Add the noodles and cook until barely softened, about 5 minutes. Remove the noodles. Add the cabbage and cook for 4 minutes. Remove the cabbage.

4. In the large bowl, combine the still-warm potatoes, noodles, and cabbage with the butter mixture and all but 2 tablespoons (12 g) each of the Parmesan and fontina cheeses. Season with salt and pepper.

5. Transfer the noodle mixture to a large baking dish, (greased with oil of choice) add the vegetable broth, and top with the remaining 2 tablespoons (12 g) each Parmesan and fontina cheeses and the bread crumbs. Bake until golden brown and delicious, about 35 minutes. Garnish with the chopped parsley.

YIELD: 4 servings

Fideo

This dish is an interesting example of the Moorish influence on the south of Spain. Because Spain had a smaller noodle culture than most countries, it took the ingenuity of some Muslim farmers to make paella (a nationally treasured rice dish) with noodles and whatever else was available. This paella-like dish shows off that old adage "what grows together, goes together." You don't have to stock your pantry with Spanish fideo noodles, Spanish olive oil, Spanish chorizo, and Spanish peppers, but it can be a fun shopping excursion and dinner party project for the whole family. Pour some wine from Rioja for the adults, and you are almost in Spain.

INGREDIENTS

- ¼ cup (60 ml) cold-pressed, extra-virgin olive oil
- 1 Vidalia onion, diced
- 1 pound (454 g) fideo (you can also use angel hair or capellini pasta broken into 2-inch [5 cm] pieces)
- 2 fresh Espelette peppers, diced (you can also use another sweet pepper such as fresh Padrón peppers or jarred piquillo peppers)
- ½ head garlic, minced
- ½ cup (50 g) olives
- 2 tablespoons (14 g) diced dried chorizo
- 1 teaspoon pimentón or paprika
- 4 sprigs fresh herbs, leaves and stems divided and chopped (choose your favorite: cilantro, parsley)
- 4 cups (940 ml) vegetable broth
- 1 pound (454 g) tomatoes, chopped
  Salt and pepper, to taste
- 2 tablespoons (12 g) grated manchego or Parmesan cheese

OTHER STUFF

9 x 13-inch (23 x 33 cm) roasting pan

HOW TO

1. Preheat the oven to 400°F (200°C, or gas mark 6).

2. Place the roasting pan on the stove over medium-high heat. Add the olive oil and onion and cook for 5 minutes. Add the pasta and cook until slightly browned, about 3 minutes. Now add the peppers, garlic, olives, chorizo, pimentón, and herb stems and cook until a nice, even red color is achieved, about 3 minutes. Add the broth and tomatoes and season with salt and pepper.

3. Bake until golden brown and delicious, about 35 minutes. Garnish with the chopped herb leaves and cheese.

YIELD: 4 servings

THAT'S THE PITS
When Chef cooks with olives, he leaves the pits in because they give the dish a lot of flavor. If he's having kids over for dinner he usually takes the pits out before he serves them, but it's always good to ask before you bite into one. Otherwise: "Ouch!"

noodlecat

Lasagna

Like Garfield, I love lasagna. It's such a satisfying dish to make and enjoy. There are lots of ways to make lasagna an expression of your personal taste: Make the ragù (meat suace) with turkey or tofu. Add a layer of blanched spinach, sautéed mushrooms, or sliced prosciutto. Replace the béchamel with ricotta and cream (shortcut!). Personally, I like to add more noodles than the average lasagna builder. It helps hold the lasagna together better.

INGREDIENTS

2 recipes Fresh Pasta Dough (page 39), rolled and cut into 4 x 2-inch (10 x 5 cm) pieces, or 1½ pounds (680 g) no-boil lasagna sheets

Cold-pressed, extra-virgin olive oil, as needed

5 tomatoes, sliced

4 sprigs basil, chopped

2 cups (200 g) grated Parmesan cheese

3 cups (750 g) Catcher's Italian Meat Sauce (page 69) or your favorite tomato sauce

2 cups (220 g) sliced fresh mozzarella

1 cup (120 g) sliced grilled zucchini

1 cup (100 g) sliced grilled eggplant

3 cups (705 ml) Béchamel Sauce (recipe follows on page 62)

OTHER STUFF

Pasta pot with strainer

Large bowl filled with ice and water

Parchment paper

9 x 13-inch (23 x 33 cm) baking dish

Aluminum foil

HOW TO

1. If using fresh pasta dough, fill a large pot with water and season with salt until it tastes like seawater. Bring to a simmer over medium heat. Working in batches of four or five, cook the pasta sheets for 5 minutes, until softened but not cooked through. Transfer the blanched pasta sheets to a large bowl of ice and water to cool completely. Reserve ½ cup (120 ml) of the pasta water. Drain the cooled noodles, toss lightly with olive oil, and layer between parchment papers.

STOP (IF YOU WANT TO)! You can store the blanched pasta sheets in the refrigerator until dinner or freeze them for up to 1 month for later use.

2. Preheat the oven to 350°F (180°C, or gas mark 4) and oil the baking dish.

3. Build the lasagna. Each layer should be thin—about ¼ inch (6 mm). Be creative with the order of your layers. Start with a layer of fresh tomato, basil, and Parmesan. Top with a layer of noodles. Add a layer of sauce and Parmesan and top with a layer of noodles. Add a layer of mozzarella and top with noodles. Add a layer of vegetables and top with noodles. Add a layer of béchamel and top with noodles. Begin again with the layer of sauce, following the same pattern until the noodles are gone, ending with the noodles. Add a thin layer of sauce, the remaining tomatoes, and the remaining Parmesan and mozzarella. Garnish with basil

4. Bake, covered with aluminum foil, for 25 minutes. Uncover and cook an additional 25 minutes. Allow to cool for 20 minutes before serving.

YIELD: 8 servings

Start with a layer of fresh tomato, basil, and Parmesan.

Each layer should be thin.

Top with a thin layer of sauce, cheese, tomatoes, and herbs.

Béchamel Sauce

I like to make béchamel the fast way at home. In a classic recipe, you would melt butter, make a roux, add the milk and nutmeg, whisk, strain, and so on. We do ours sort of backward. It requires less time and attention and is still delicious.

INGREDIENTS

- 3   tablespoons (24 g) all-purpose flour
- 1   teaspoon kosher salt
- 1   teaspoon ground nutmeg
- 3   tablespoons (42 g) salted butter, at room temperature
- 3   tablespoons (45 ml) cold-pressed, extra-virgin olive oil
- 4   cups (940 ml) whole milk

OTHER STUFF

Small bowl
Small saucepan
Whisk
Blender
Strainer
Parchment paper

HOW TO

1. In the bowl, mix together the flour, salt, nutmeg, butter, and olive oil.

2. In the saucepan over medium-low heat, bring the milk to a simmer. Whisking constantly, slowly add the flour mixture. The milk will thicken almost immediately. Simmer for an additional 2 minutes.

3. Transfer the milk mixture to a blender. Blend until smooth and strain into a bowl. To prevent the "milk skin" that naturally forms on cooling milk, float a piece of parchment paper on top of the milk as it cools.

YIELD: 1 quart (940 ml)

PERSONAL PAN LASAGNA
Sometimes I ask Chef for a little pan to build my own personal lasagna. We call it a lasagnette. I can put anything I want between the layers. (Chef says there has to be some vegetables!) My little lasagna only has three or four layers, but one of my favorites is from Mark Ladner at Del Posto in New York City, made famous by 100 layers!

noodlecat

Noodlecat in Greece

The Italians aren't the only ones who had the awesome idea of layering noodles and other delicious things. In Greece, they call it *pastitsio,* and they use hollow noodles kind of like ziti. The noodles are layered with a meat sauce and a cheese sauce and then baked. The house smells really good, like it does when you are making lasagna.

We don't talk about the Greeks when it comes to pasta nearly as much as we talk about the Italians, but Greece has lots of pastas and a long noodle-y history. There's mention of something a lot like pasta as far back as the second century. That's a long time ago.

Today in Greece you are most likely to see *hilopites.* The dough is made with eggs and rolled out into long, thin strips like linguine. Then the dough is cut into squares and dried. You can serve the pasta with lots of different things. It makes a great Greek chicken soup and it's really good with butter and cheese, too.

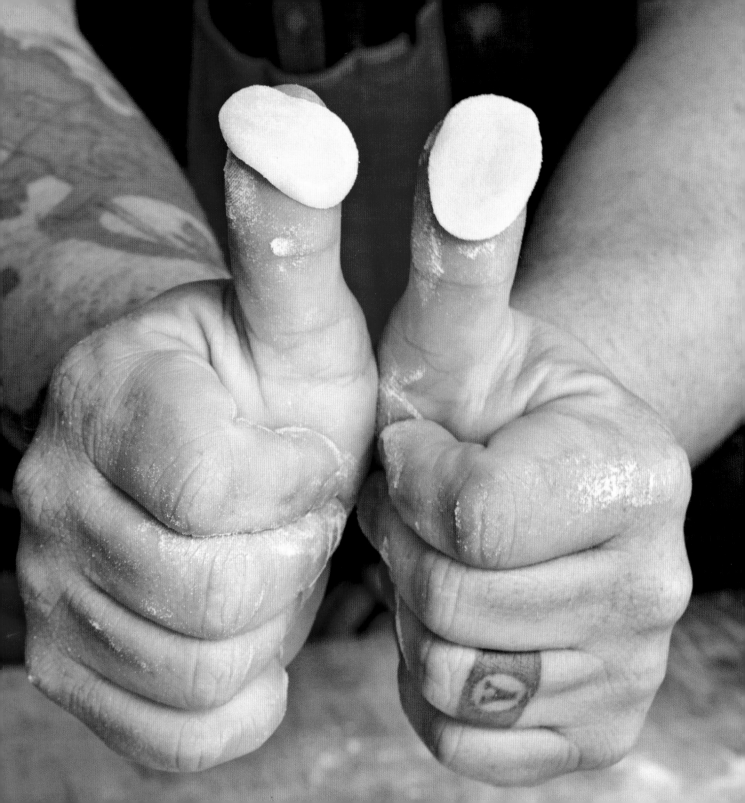

Chapter 5

Gnocchi Time

What is gnocchi? Gnocchi are so different from most of the noodles we eat. They are voluptuous and pillowy because there isn't much gluten development. I think for a pasta to be gnocchi, it has to have egg, flour, and a third major component. That third component can be potato or ricotta or even ground beef. Meatballs are gnocchi!

Like so many recipes, gnocchi recipes are frugal. They are designed to feed lots of people with a minimum of luxury ingredients. We make potato gnocchi a lot at home. It really shows off sauces well. Catcher's favorite is the meaty ragù on page 66.

There's also a polenta gnocchi in this chapter. It doesn't really follow the rules of gnocchi because it doesn't have a third major ingredient, but the Italians have been calling it gnocchi for years, and you can't argue with the Italians when it comes to pasta.

Classic Potato Gnocchi with Catcher's Italian Meat Sauce

Think of toothy fresh linguine as a nice chewy Parisian baguette bread and airy potato gnocchi as tender Southern biscuits. When you are making linguine or a baguette you are trying to develop gluten, which gives them their structure. With gnocchi and biscuits, though, you don't want lots of gluten to develop. To prevent it, be careful not to knead the dough more than absolutely necessary. This also helps develop the nice toothy bite often referred to as al dente.

INGREDIENTS

2	Idaho potatoes
1½	to 2 cups (188 to 250 g) organic all-purpose flour
3	large organic eggs, beaten
1	recipe Catcher's Italian Meat Sauce (recipe follows on page 69)
1	tablespoon (15 ml) cold-pressed, extra-virgin olive oil
6	tablespoons (24 g) chopped fresh herbs (choose your favorite: oregano, parsley, basil)
2	tablespoons (14 g) toasted bread crumbs
2	tablespoons (12 g) grated Parmesan cheese

OTHER STUFF

Cake tester (optional)

Food mill or potato ricer or masher

Stand mixer with paddle attachment (optional)

Wooden cutting board

Cookie sheet

Large saucepan

Pasta pot with strainer

HOW TO

1. Preheat the oven to 325°F (170°C, or gas mark 3) and roast the potatoes until fully cooked through, about 50 minutes.

Tip: A cake tester makes a great potato tester. When it goes through the potato without resistance, the potato is done. Allow the potatoes to cool to room temperature. Boiling the potatoes is also a perfectly fine option, just skin them and boil until a cake tester or toothpick goes through without resistance.

2. Split the potatoes and scoop out all the flesh, leaving all the skin behind. Use the food mill, potato ricer, or potato masher to mash the potatoes.

3. Combine the potatoes with 1½ cups (188 g) of the flour in the stand mixer using a dough hook or on a cutting board. If using the cutting board, shape the potato-flour mixture into a volcano shape to contain the eggs during the mixing process. Add the eggs to the mixer or "volcano" and stir until just combined. The dough should be slightly sticky, but if it is too sticky, add more flour. Shape the dough into a rectangle and allow it to rest for 15 minutes. (See photos, page 68.)

4. Dust a wooden cutting board with flour. Cut a 1-inch (2.5 cm) wide piece from the dough rectangle and roll the piece of dough between your hands on the cutting board to make a long cylinder or snake about as thick as a roll of quarters. Cut the cylinder into 1-inch (2.5 cm) pieces. Place on a flour-dusted cookie sheet and store in the freezer. Fancy home cooks can fork it instead of a knife and roll them on a gnocchi board for that classic look.

STOP (IF YOU WANT)! Gnocchi can be made in advance and frozen for 2 to 3 months until you are ready to use them.

5. In a large saucepan, warm the meat sauce over low heat.

6. Fill a large pot with water and season with salt until it tastes like seawater. Bring to a boil over high heat. Blanch eight gnocchi at a time, for about 7 minutes per batch. Gnocchi are done when they bob to the top and float there for a minute. Transfer each batch of gnocchi to the sauce and simmer for an additional 3 minutes to allow the noodle and sauce to become one.

7. Garnish with the olive oil, herbs, bread crumbs, and Parmesan.

YIELD: 6 servings

Form the potato-flour mixture into a volcano shape to contain the eggs during the mixing process.

Add the eggs to the "volcano" and stir until just combined. The dough should be slightly sticky.

Shape the dough into a rectangle and allow it to rest for 15 minutes.

Cut a 1-inch (2.5 cm) wide piece from the dough rectangle.

Roll the dough between your hands on the cutting board to make a long cylinder or snake about as thick as a roll of quarters.

Cut the cylinder into 1-inch (2.5 cm) pieces. Place on a flour-dusted cookie sheet and store in the freezer.

Catcher's Italian Meat Sauce

Sometimes we call this "*The Ragù*." A traditional ragù Bolognese would have veal and pork in addition to the beef, but this is Catcher's favorite, so he gets what he likes. The secret to this dish is adding the ingredients at specific times and letting the flavors develop and layer. It's a little bit of food magic.

INGREDIENTS

½ pound (227 g) pancetta or lightly smoked bacon
1 tablespoon (15 ml) cold-pressed, extra-virgin olive oil
1 Vidalia onion, chopped
1 stalk celery, chopped
1 carrot, chopped
½ bulb fennel, chopped
5 cloves garlic
2 tablespoons (8 g) chopped fresh herbs (choose your favorite: oregano, parsley, basil)
½ pound (227 g) 70% lean grass-fed beef
½ teaspoon anchovy paste
1 cup (235 ml) dry Italian red wine
1 cup (235 ml) whole organic milk
2 cups (500 g) tomato passato

OTHER STUFF

Food processor
Sauté pan
Potato masher

HOW TO

1. Combine the pancetta, olive oil, onion, celery, carrot, fennel, garlic, and herbs in the food processor. Pulse until finely chopped and well combined. (This mixture is often known as the soffrito.) Sauté the soffrito slowly in a pan over low heat, stirring often, approximately 25 minutes. If you'd like to, you can roast the soffrito first covered, then uncovered, to achieve maximum vegetable flavor extraction.

2. Add the beef and anchovy paste to the soffrito and increase the heat to high. Lightly brown the meat, using a potato masher to achieve a fine texture.

3. Add the wine and cook over medium-high heat until 90 percent of the wine has evaporated. Add the milk and continue to cook over medium-high heat until 70 percent of the milk has evaporated. (It will appear to curdle. This is just part of the magic.) Add the tomato passato, lower the heat, and simmer for 40 minutes.

YIELD: 1 quart (940 ml)

> Take the time to develop the flavors in this sauce. Adding ingredients at specific times allows foods magic to happen. It's just sauce, but it can be great sauce.

Chef Says

Ricotta Gnocchi with Squash and Garlic Sauce

I love using as few dishes as possible in the kitchen. You already have water boiling for the pasta. Why not use it to cook the squash and garlic, too? If you time it right, you can pull everything out at once.

INGREDIENTS

2 cups (220 g) diced squash

5 cloves garlic, halved

1 recipe Ricotta Gnocchi (recipe follows)

2 tablespoons (28 g) salted butter

1 lemon, zested and juiced

3 tablespoons (12 g) chopped parsley, divided

1 tablespoon (6 g) grated Parmesan cheese

1 tablespoon (5 g) sliced almonds

OTHER STUFF

Pasta pot with strainer

Large saucepan

HOW TO

1. Bring water to a boil in the pasta pot over medium-high heat. Add the squash and garlic and cook for 5 minutes. Add the gnocchi, 8 at a time, to the pasta pot. Cook each batch of gnocchi until they float for 1 minute, about 5 minutes.

2. In the saucepan over medium-high heat, melt the butter. Transfer the gnocchi, squash, and garlic to the saucepan and cook until lightly browned. Add ¼ cup (60 ml) of the pasta water, the lemon juice and zest, and 1½ tablespoons (6 g) of the parsley to the saucepan. Simmer for an additional 3 minutes. Garnish with the remaining 1½ tablespoons (6 g) parsley, Parmesan, and almonds.

YIELD: 4 servings

Ricotta Gnocchi

In texture these are more like Amish dumplings than Italian potato gnocchi—so soft and delicious. I recommend using the full amount of flour initially to ensure successful gnocchi, but remember, the less flour you use, the lighter and airier the gnocchi. Once you get comfortable with the recipe you can experiment.

INGREDIENTS
- 2 **large organic eggs**
- 1 **pound (454 g) ricotta cheese**
- 2 **cups (200 g) grated Parmesan cheese**
  Pinch of nutmeg
  Pinch of salt
- 1½ **cups (188 g) all-purpose organic flour,**
  plus more as needed

OTHER STUFF
Stand mixer

HOW TO

1. In the stand mixer, beat the eggs until just combined. Add the ricotta and Parmesan cheeses, nutmeg, and salt and blend. Add the flour in three batches, mixing until just incorporated. The mixture should be slightly sticky to the touch. If the dough is too sticky, add some more flour.

WAIT! Allow the gnocchi dough to rest for 15 minutes. Or freeze for 2 to 3 months for use later.

2. Shape the gnocchi into balls just smaller than a golf ball. Dust with flour and refrigerate.

WAIT! Allow the gnocchi to rest in the refrigerator for 10 minutes.

YIELD: About 30 gnocchi

PRACTICE, PRACTICE, PRACTICE
It takes practice to make yummy noodles. The more often you make—and eat—gnocchi, the more delicious they will be. Each time, you can use a little less flour, making them lighter and lighter until they almost float away!

noodlecat

Noodlecat in France

There aren't many noodles that come from France. I guess they are too busy baking bread! But the French do have their own version of gnocchi. They call it *gnocchi à la Parisienne*, or "gnocchi of Paris." They look a lot like the traditional Italian gnocchi that Chef taught us how to make in this book, but they are made differently. There's no potato. Instead, you make the gnocchi of Paris with just water, butter, flour, and eggs, plus any other stuff you want, like cheese and herbs. (Even better, you can use the same kind of dough to make dessert, too.)

Instead of rolling the gnocchi, you put it in a pastry bag and squeeze the dough right into the boiling water, using a knife to cut it into little pieces. Just like their Italian cousins, they are tender and light, like pillows of pasta.

But even though there aren't a lot of other noodles in the traditional French kitchen, people still love pasta. In fact, noodles are a sign of love in France. It's a tradition for kids to give a *collier de nouilles*—a necklace they make out of pretty pasta shapes—to their mothers for Mother's Day.

Gnocchi alla Romana

Sometimes we make this dish just as it's written here. Other times I make soft polenta to serve with supper one night and I save the leftovers to make this dish later in the week. All you have to do is add the flour, cheese, and eggs. Cooking in large batches and using all the leftovers is something we do in the restaurant. It makes a lot of sense at home, too.

INGREDIENTS

- 6 cups (1410 ml) whole organic milk
- 3 tablespoons (42 g) salted butter
  Pinch of ground nutmeg
  Salt and pepper, to taste
- 2 cups (280 g) polenta or semolina
- 1 tablespoon (8 g) all-purpose organic flour
- 2 cups (200 g) grated Pecorino Romano or Parmesan cheese, divided
- 2 large organic eggs, lightly beaten
- 1 cup (235 ml) Basic Tomato Sauce (page 52) or your favorite tomato sauce

OTHER STUFF

Two square (9-inch, or 23 cm each) baking dishes
Medium saucepan
Whisk
Spatula
Plastic wrap
Round cookie cutter

HOW TO

1. Preheat the oven to 350°F (180°C, or gas mark 4) and grease two baking dishes.

2. In a medium saucepan over medium-high heat, combine the milk, butter, nutmeg, and salt and pepper. Add the polenta in a slow, steady stream while whisking vigorously. Reduce the heat to low and cook until the polenta has thickened slightly, about 10 minutes. Remove the polenta from the heat and stir in the flour and 1⅔ cups (165 g) of the cheese. Allow the mixture to cool to room temperature and then stir in the eggs.

3. Pour the mixture into one baking dish and smooth the top with a spatula. Cover with plastic wrap and cool in the refrigerator.

4. Using the round cookie cutter, cut the cooled polenta into circles. Layer the rounds in concentric circles in the other baking dish. Top with the tomato sauce and the remaining ⅓ cup (35 g) cheese. Bake until golden brown and delicious, about 25 minutes.

YIELD: 4 servings

> If you are using an heirloom variety of polenta, good for you. Just follow the package cooking instructions before adding the cheese and eggs. Some types of heirloom polentas can take as long as 3 hours to cook.
>
> *Chef Says*

Meatballs Are Gnocchi!

In the United States, we've messed up the sacred union of meat and bread known as the "meatball." Traditionally, a meatball is at least a 50:50 ratio of meat to bread. And because it's bound with egg, it's a type of gnocchi. As with all gnocchi, the texture is key. You are looking for tender, not chewy, so be mindful not to overmix.

GET THE SCOOP
The ice cream scoop isn't just for ice cream. It makes perfectly sized meatballs, too. Another trick I learned from Chef: Dipping your hands in water before rolling the meatballs makes everything less sticky.

noodlecat

INGREDIENTS

- 1 Vidalia onion, diced
- 4 cloves garlic, minced
- 1 red bell pepper, cored, seeded, and diced
- 2 cups plus 2 tablespoons (500 ml) cold-pressed, extra-virgin olive oil, divided
- 2 cups (200 g) diced bread or bread crumbs
- 2 large organic eggs
- ¼ cup (58 g) ricotta cheese
- ½ cup (50 g) grated Parmesan cheese
- 2 tablespoons (4 g) sliced Italian herbs (choose your favorite: parsley, oregano, basil)
- 1 pound (454 g) ground pork
  Salt and pepper, to taste
  Organic all-purpose flour, as needed
- 2 cups (470 ml) Basic Tomato Sauce (page 52) or your favorite tomato sauce

OTHER STUFF

Small saucepan with cover
Large bowls
Food-handling gloves
Large, heavy-bottomed sauté pan
9 x 13-inch (23 x 33 cm) baking dish

> I like to check the seasoning before I fry all the meatballs. Just make a little patty from the meatball mixture, sear it in olive oil until cooked through, and give it a taste. Does it need more salt or pepper? Now is the best time to add it.

Chef Says

HOW TO

1. In a small saucepan over low heat, sauté the onion, garlic and pepper in 2 tablespoons (30 ml) of the olive oil. Cook slowly, covered, stirring occasionally, similar to cooking soffrito (see page 69).

2. In a large bowl, soak the bread crumbs in water to cover for 1 minute. Strain out the excess liquid.

3. In a separate large bowl, beat the eggs, and then add the ricotta, Parmesan, sautéed onion mixture, and herbs. Mix thoroughly. Add the meat and soaked bread crumbs. It's easiest to don gloves and mix the meat and bread crumbs in with your hands. Season with salt and pepper.

4. Shape the meatballs into balls slightly larger than a golf ball, but much smaller than a tennis ball.

WAIT! Refrigerate the meatballs until chilled. This ensures a more even searing.

5. In the large sauté pan over medium-high heat, heat the remaining 2 cups (470 ml) olive oil. Preheat the oven to 350°F (180°C, or gas mark 4). Dust the meatballs lightly with flour. Spread the tomato sauce in a baking dish.

6. Working with batches of 5 meatballs, brown the meatballs on all sides in the olive oil. Once browned, transfer the meatballs to the baking dish. When you are finished sautéing, discard the olive oil, reserving any pan drippings or browned meat remaining in the sauté pan. Add to the baking dish and bake for 20 minutes, until cooked through.

YIELD: 4 servings

Chapter 6

Saucy

When you make as much pasta as we do, you learn that certain noodles go best with traditional sauces. In fact, different noodles were designed for different sauces. Sometimes you want fresh noodles. Sometimes you want dry noodles. Long, thick noodles are best for hardy sauces. Thin, dried noodles go great with olive-oil based sauces. And short, craggy shapes are perfect for chunky sauces. Shapes such as orecchiette are ideal for carrying bits of sausage and greens from the plate to your mouth.

But that doesn't mean you can't experiment. Knowing your noodles—and the other ingredients in your pantry—is the first step to cooking a great meal with your family.

Lulu's Not-Linguine and Clams

One time, I took Louisiana and Catcher into the kitchen at the restaurant to make soup. I gave both kids a small saucepan and let them grab any ingredients they wanted. Lulu took a bunch of blanched French fries and clams. That's it. I steamed open the clams and she ate them all, licking the bowl clean. A couple of years later, she tried a true bucatini and clams in Italy. She just went bonkers for it. Now we make our own version of her favorite at home.

INGREDIENTS

24 whole, live littleneck clams, purged and rinsed
1 head garlic, cloves peeled and smashed
6 tablespoons (84 g) salted butter, divided
1 pound (454 g) bucatini
1 cup (235 ml) white wine
¼ cup (16 g) chopped fresh herbs, divided (choose your favorites: parsley, oregano)
¼ cup (25 g) toasted bread crumbs
1 tablespoon (15 ml) cold-pressed, extra-virgin olive oil
  Crushed red pepper flakes
  Crispy garlic and shallot chips (available at Asian and Middle Eastern markets)
  Crusty bread

OTHER STUFF

  Pasta pot with strainer
  Big saucepan with cover
  Serving plates

HOW TO

1. Fill the pasta pot with water and season with salt until it tastes like seawater. Bring to a boil over high heat.

2. In the big saucepan, combine the clams, garlic, and 3 tablespoons (42 g) of the butter. Cover and cook over medium-low heat for 5 minutes to sauté the garlic.

3. Add the bucatini to the saucepan of boiling water and cook for 7 minutes. Drain the bucatini, reserving ½ cup (120 ml) of the pasta water.

4. Add the wine and 2 tablespoons (8 g) of the herbs to the clams and cook uncovered for 5 minutes to reduce the liquid. (Most of the clams should be open by now. If they aren't, don't fret. You can add ½ cup [120 ml] pasta water, cover, and cook until the clams open, up to 10 minutes. After 10 minutes, discard any clams that aren't open.) Transfer the open clams to serving plates.

5. Add the remaining 3 tablespoons (42 g) butter and cooked bucatini to the clam sauce in the pan. Simmer over low heat until the sauce and bucatini become one, about 3 minutes. Transfer to the serving plates, garnish with the bread crumbs, and drizzle with the olive oil.

6. Bring the red pepper flakes, remaining 2 tablespoons (16 g) herbs, and crispy garlic and shallot chips to the table so everyone can season and crunchify their own dinner. Don't forget the spoon and the scarpetta.

YIELD: 6 servings

WHY WOULD YOU WANT TO EAT A SHOE?
In Italy, everyone loves to eat 'scarpetta,' which is weird because *scarpetta* means a 'small shoe' or 'heel.' But before I tried to eat my sneaker, someone told me scarpetta also means a crusty piece of bread you use to mop up every last bit of sauce. It's even better than licking your plate.

noodlecat

Spaghetti and Lobster

Larger chain restaurants that are using frozen, fake, or endangered spiny lobsters with chili and cream frequently ruin this Venetian pasta dish. In its essence, it's a lobster-worship-worthy recipe. You only need one lobster to feed your family, so this dish isn't a huge splurge. But it's still lobster, so it feels like a celebration even if it's just a Tuesday night dinner. This recipe also uses the "bones" of the lobster to turn your Basic Tomato Sauce (page 52) into something special.

INGREDIENTS

1½ pound live lobster, cut into 6 pieces

1 tablespoon (15 ml) cold-pressed, extra-virgin olive oil
Salt, to taste

¼ cup (60 ml) cognac, vodka, or white wine

5 cups (1175 ml) Basic Tomato Sauce (page 52), or your favorite sauce, puréed until smooth

1 bunch basil, leaves thinly sliced and stems tied with kitchen string

1 pound (454 g) spaghetti

2 tablespoons (28 g) salted butter

OTHER STUFF

Pasta pot with strainer
Roasting pan
Kitchen string

HOW TO

1. Preheat the oven to 350°F (180°C, or gas mark 4). Fill the pasta pot with water and season with salt until it tastes like seawater. Bring to a boil over high heat.

2. Toss the lobster pieces with the olive oil and salt to coat and place in the roasting pan. Roast until medium-rare, about 5 minutes. Remove from the oven and add the cognac to the hot pan. Wait 2 minutes to allow some alcohol to evaporate. Add the tomato sauce and basil stems and simmer on the stove top over low heat for 10 minutes.

3. Cook the spaghetti according to the package instructions.

4. Remove the lobster and basil from the sauce. Remove the lobster meat from the shells and chop the meat. Return the meat to the sauce; discard the shells and basil stems. Transfer the spaghetti to the sauce and simmer everything together for 2 minutes. Stir the basil leaves and butter into the pasta.

YIELD: 4 servings

> If your great fear of live lobsters is of Annie Hall proportions, have the fishmonger cut it for you. Ask for the lobster to be cut into six pieces: the tail, the claws and knuckles, and the body (a.k.a. 'the bones'). You'll use every piece in this recipe.

Chef Says

Little Ears with Kale

It's easy to see why this pasta is called orecchiette, an Italian name that translates to "little ears." That's what these little noodles look like. The "ears" are perfect for holding a chunky sauce. The classic orecchiette recipe calls for spicy chiles, garlic, bread crumbs, and bitter broccoli rabe, but Team Sawyer is really into kale. The south of Italy, just around the ankle and below on the proverbial boot of the peninsula, is a great grain-growing region. Really, the best copper-extruded artisanal dried pasta comes from there, although now great commercially produced orecchiette is available.

This is a great activity to do with the kids. You make the dough and cut the disks. The kids form the shapes, and you finish the sauce.

INGREDIENTS

- 2 tablespoons (30 ml) cold-pressed, extra-virgin olive oil, divided
- 1 cup (110 g) crumbled Italian sausage, casing removed
- 1 clove garlic, diced
- 1 tablespoon (4 g) chopped parsley, divided
- 1 pound (454 g) orecchiette, homemade (recipe follows), or store-bought
- ½ pound (227 g) sliced kale
- ½ cup (50 g) toasted bread crumbs
- ½ cup (50 g) grated Parmesan cheese
- Pinch of crushed red pepper flakes

OTHER STUFF

- Pasta pot with strainer
- Medium saucepan
- Potato masher

HOW TO

1. Fill the pasta pot with water and season with salt until it tastes like seawater. Bring to a boil over high heat.

2. In the saucepan over medium-high heat, heat 1 tablespoon (15 ml) of the olive oil and sauté the sausage until just cooked through, using the potato masher to get an even consistency. Add the garlic and ½ tablespoon (2 g) of the parsley and continue to sauté.

3. Add the homemade orecchiette to the pasta pot and cook for 6 minutes (or follow the package instructions for store-bought orecchiette). Add the kale to the pasta pot and cook for an additional 4 minutes.

4. Transfer the greens and pasta with some water clinging to them to the saucepan with the sausage. Reduce the heat to low and simmer until a sauce forms, about 2 minutes. Remove from the heat and stir in the remaining 1 tablespoon (15 ml) olive oil and remaining ½ tablespoon (2 g) parsley. Garnish with the bread crumbs, Parmesan, and red pepper flakes.

YIELD: 4 servings

Homemade Orecchiette

This is our everyday orecchiette recipe, but you can also easily incorporate whole grains. Substitute up to half of the all-purpose and semolina flours with whole wheat, faro, or buckwheat flours.

INGREDIENTS
  1   **cup (125 g) all-purpose organic flour**
  1   **cup (125 g) semolina flour**
1¼ cups (295 ml) warm water

OTHER STUFF
  Stand mixer with a dough hook attachment
  Knife

HOW TO
1. Combine all the ingredients in the stand mixer and mix for 15 minutes to develop the gluten. The dough shouldn't be sticky when you are done.

WAIT! Cover the dough with plastic wrap or under a damp towel and allow to rest at room temperature for 30 minutes.

2. Using your hands, divide the dough into pieces and roll each piece into a dowel shape, about the diameter of nickel. Cut the dowels into ¼-inch (6 mm) thick disks. Using your thumb, press each disk flat, and then pull your thumb toward you to curl the pasta like an ear.

YIELD: 1½ pounds (680 g)

GET OUT YOUR BIG BENT THUMB
These little ears are my favorite to make. They are easy—you just need your thumb!— and we can make lots and lots and then freeze them for later.

Roll a portion of the dough into a dowel shape, about the diameter of a nickel.

Cut the dowel into ¼-inch (6 mm) thick disks.

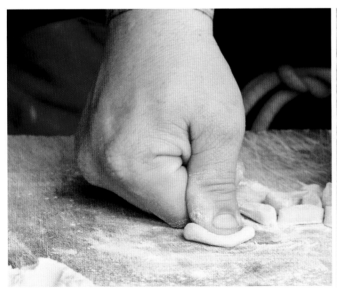

Using your thumb, press each disk flat, then pull your thumb toward you to curl the pasta like an ear.

The finished orecchiette look just like little ears.

Bucatini all'Amatriciana

This recipe is from the town of Amatrice and is often referred to as pasta Amatrice. However, this classic sauce is more commonly associated with Rome, where it is known as all'Amatriciana. It is intensely flavored with pork, tomato, and pecorino, and bucatini, with its slightly thicker than spaghetti shape and hollow center, is the perfect pairing for it.

INGREDIENTS

- 1 pound (454 g) bucatini
- 1 cup (80 g) diced guanciale, pancetta, or bacon
- 2 cups (360 g) crushed tomatoes
- 1½ cups (150 g) grated pecorino cheese
- 1 tablespoon (15 ml) cold-pressed, extra-virgin olive oil
- Pinch of crushed red pepper flakes

OTHER STUFF

Pasta pot with strainer
Medium saucepan

HOW TO

1. Fill the pasta pot with water and season with salt until it tastes like seawater. Bring to a boil over high heat. Add the bucatini and cook according to the package directions until al dente. Drain and reserve ½ cup (120 ml) of the pasta water.

2. In a medium saucepan over high heat, combine the reserved pasta water and the guanciale. Cook until the water has evaporated, about 3 minutes, and then continue to sauté the guanciale until lightly browned, about 4 minutes. Add the tomatoes and reduce the heat to simmer the sauce until the bucatini is ready, probably about 3 minutes.

3. Add the bucatini, with some water still clinging to the noodles, to the sauce and continue to simmer until the sauce sticks to the pasta, about 2 minutes. Remove from the heat and stir in the cheese, olive oil, and red pepper flakes.

YIELD: 4 servings

WHERE'S THE SALT?
Chef taught me that a little salt can make things taste better. But no salt will be necessary, because seasoned pasta water + salty pig parts + salty cheese = perfectly seasoned noodles.

noodlecat

Garlic and Parm Mazeman Ramen

Mazeman style of ramen is very popular in Tokyo and New York City right now. It is the most modern widely accepted derivation of the classic ramen bowl known as neo-ramen.

We like the Mazeman style because we can think about it more globally. It could be a Japanese-style macaroni and cheese, like this recipe, or a tomato and mussels seafood stew, barbecued brisket and beef drippings, or saffron and Spanish chorizo. You can also get a little crazy and mush up some uni and softened miso butter Santa Barbara, California style. It's a very liberating style of ramen, allowing you to cook fusion any way you'd like.

INGREDIENTS

- 1 cup (165 g) cooked rice
- 1 cup (90 g) plus 1 tablespoon (5 g) bonito flakes, divided
- 5 cloves garlic
- 1 tablespoon (5 g) dried shiitake mushroom powder
- 4 cups (940 ml) water
- 2 tablespoons (30 ml) soy sauce
- 1 tablespoon (15 ml) MAAGI liquid seasoning or Worcestershire sauce
- 1 teaspoon cracked black pepper
- 2 cups (200 g) grated Parmesan cheese
- 2 tablespoons (30 g) shiro miso
- 2 pounds (908 g) thick, curly ramen
- ¼ cup (25 g) sliced scallion
- 1 cup (180 g) blanched spinach
- 6 sheets dried kombu
- 1 tablespoon (5 g) crispy garlic chips (available at Asian and Middle Eastern markets)
- ½ cup (40 g) chopped cooked bacon
- 1 recipe 6½-Minute Eggs (page 104)

OTHER STUFF

- Large saucepan
- Blender
- Pasta pot with strainer
- Serving bowls

Tip: The Japanese think about miso as a living, breathing, ingredient and rarely add it during the cooking process; instead, they add it just prior to serving, preserving the restorative properties reputed by miso maniacs. This is akin to how the Italians add their estate's super-fresh primo olive oil only at the end of the cooking process.

HOW TO

1. In the large saucepan over medium-low heat, combine the rice, 1 cup (90 g) of the bonito flakes, garlic, mushroom powder, water, soy sauce, MAAGI liquid seasoning, and pepper. Simmer for 10 minutes. Transfer to the blender, add the Parmesan, and purée until smooth. Add the miso and purée until smooth. Keep the mixture warm.

2. Fill the pasta pot with water and season with salt until it tastes like seawater. Bring to a boil over high heat. Add the ramen and cook for 50 seconds if using dried ramen, 3 minutes if using fresh ramen, and 5 minutes if using fresh-frozen ramen. Drain the ramen and rinse under hot water to remove more alkaline. Toss the ramen with the warm sauce.

3. Divide the ramen evenly among 6 bowls and garnish with the scallion, spinach, kombu, crispy garlic chips, bacon, eggs, and remaining 1 tablespoon (5 g) bonito flakes.

YIELD: 6 servings

Chapter 7

Slurps

I have an Eastern European background, and soup is big part of that culture. The easiest way to think about eating more vegetables is to have more soup. As long as you have good seasoning, good sautéing technique, and good vegetables, your soup will taste good.

Amelia hates most soups, but she loves ramen, which is just a Japanese soup. We have been ramen-heads forever. It was one of our favorite meals when we lived in New York, and we even made a pilgrimage to the ramen mecca of the world, Japan. When we moved back to Cleveland, there wasn't really any ramen around. We wanted to introduce Catcher, Lulu, and other Noodle Kids—and all of Cleveland—to ramen. That's why we opened our ramen shop, Noodlecat. Making ramen can be a lifetime endeavor, and everyone has an opinion on what is "authentic" Japanese ramen. We're still learning; we're on our fifth iteration of broth and noodles. We're not traditionalists. Our ramen is a mash-up of what we get here in Ohio, what tradition has taught us, and what we love.

Tofu and Udon Soup

Soup has many forms in Japan: *suimono*, "things to sip," is often served without a spoon; *zosui* is a homey stew often made with rice; and there's more. This is a classic Japanese soup, but we add some tasty nontraditional edamame and a little miso. I know kombu can sound like a scary ingredient, but just do it!

INGREDIENTS

- 8 cups (2 L) water
  Instant dashi powder (optional)
- 1 sheet kombu (seaweed), soaked in water to cover overnight, soaking water reserved and kombu sliced
- 2 dried shiitake mushrooms, soaked in water to cover for 3 to 5 minutes
- ½ cup (40 g) enoki mushrooms
- 2 tablespoons (30 ml) soy sauce
- 1 tablespoon (15 ml) mirin
- 1 package (12 ounces, or 336 g) tofu, diced
- 1 teaspoon kosher salt
- ½ pound (227 g) fresh udon
- 2 tablespoons (30 g) miso
- 2 tablespoons (12 g) sliced scallion
- ½ cup (65 g) shelled snow peas or edamame

OTHER STUFF

Large saucepan
Pasta pot with strainer
Serving bowls

HOW TO

1. In the large saucepan, combine the water and instant dashi powder according to the package instructions. Add the kombu and its soaking water, shiitake and enoki mushrooms, soy sauce, mirin, tofu, and salt. Simmer the soup broth over low heat for 15 minutes. (You can remove the shiitakes after simmering.)

2. Fill the pasta pot with water and season with salt until it tastes like sea water. Bring to a boil over high heat. Cook the udon until al dente, about 5 minutes. Rinse.

3. Add the udon to the soup broth. Whisk in the miso. Divide the soup among 4 bowls and garnish with the scallion and snow peas.

YIELD: 4 servings

Cutting tofu is easy. It's the first thing I learned to cut with my own knife. To dice, cut the tofu widthwide and then lengthwise.

noodlecat

Wedding Soup (a.k.a. Meatballs and Spinach)

Team Sawyer makes soup at home all the time. Soup is a great one-pot way to get veggies into your dinner and to use up leftovers. This recipe is a little more special, but that's not why it's called "wedding soup." As with many Italian-American traditions, wedding soup is a misinterpretation. In Italian, this is "married soup," a combination of two soups enjoyed during the Christmas season around Rome.

INGREDIENTS

2	cloves garlic
1	medium carrot
½	bulb fennel
1	yellow onion
2	ribs celery
¼	cup (60 ml) cold-pressed, extra-virgin olive oil
¼	cup (60 ml) dry sherry
10	cups (2.3 L) chicken broth
1	tablespoon (2 g) oregano
1	tablespoon (5 g) diced pancetta
12	ounces (336 g) spinach, sliced
1	cup (110 g) small pasta (choose your favorite: acini de pepe, fergola, ditilini)
¼	recipe Meatballs Are Gnocchi! (page 76; make the full recipe and freeze the remaining meatballs for another meal)
3	tablespoons (18 g) grated Parmesan cheese

OTHER STUFF

Food processor (optional)

Large saucepan

HOW TO

1. Prepare the garlic, carrot, fennel, onion, and celery. You can chop, dice, or grate them, by hand or in the food processor, into whatever size you want for your soup.

2. In the large saucepan over medium heat, heat the olive oil. Add the vegetables and cook until softened but not browned, about 10 minutes. Add the sherry and cook for another 5 minutes. Add the chicken broth, oregano, and pancetta. Increase the heat and bring the soup to a boil. Add the spinach and pasta and reduce the heat to a simmer. Simmer for 5 minutes. Then add the meatballs. Serve immediately if you are in a rush or simmer for 45 minutes to 1 hour to marry the flavors. Garnish with the Parmesan.

YIELD: 4 appetizer servings

How to Throw a Ramen Party

This is the party that inspired the book you are reading right now. When we throw a Noodle Kids ramen party at Noodlecat, we do all the prep work in advance. Then everyone can have fun creating his or her own ramen recipe. The process is easy. Step 1: pick your broth; step 2: build your bowl; and step 3: add the ramen. This recipe is for six to eight, but you'll see it's easy to multiply if you have more ramen-heads around.

1 Pick Your Broth

If you make a ramen broth in advance, this ramen party will be much more fun for the cook. You can choose from Roasted Chicken Ramen Broth (page 104) or Pork Bomb Broth (page 108) or make a simple broth with instant dashi. Follow the instructions on the package.

INGREDIENTS
8 cups (2 L) of your favorite ramen broth

OTHER STUFF
Large saucepan

HOW TO
In a saucepan over low heat, bring the broth to a simmer.

YIELD: 6 to 8 servings

> There's only one rule at a Noodle Kids ramen party: You have to pick at least two veggies. (You heard me, Noodlecat!) There's a lot to choose from on the list and you can always add some of your family's favorites.
>
> *Chef Says*

2 Build Your Bowl

Your fixings are only limited by your creativity and your pantry. This ingredient list below is a sampling of our favorite fixings. Tailor them to your tastes. Don't be afraid to go wild!

INGREDIENTS

⅓   recipe 6½-Minute Eggs (page 104)
1   cup (70 g) kale, blanched
1   cup (140 g) shredded cooked chicken
1   cup (140 g) shredded cooked pork
1   cup (140 g) diced hot dogs
2   cups (280 g) diced tofu
½   cup (50 g) sliced scallion
½   cup (65 g) edamame
½   cup (35 g) cooked broccoli
½   cup (55 g) cubed cooked potatoes
¼   cup (25 g) crispy shallots (available at many Asian markets)
¼   cup (30 g) shredded carrot
¼   cup (30 g) shredded daikon
¼   cup (25 g) freeze-dried corn and peas
¼   cup (25 g) pickled ginger
¼   cup (60 ml) Crushed Peanut Dipping Sauce (page 27)
3   tablespoons (45 ml) soy sauce
3   tablespoons (45 g) miso
2   tablespoons (30 ml) fish sauce

OTHER STUFF

Bowls

HOW TO

1. Prepare your fixings and arrange them within easy reach on the table.

2. Give diners an empty bowl and let them fill it with their favorite fixings. Remember: The only rule is that you have to pick at least two vegetables!

3 Add the Ramen

The final step is to add the noodles and broth to each personalized bowl of ramen.

INGREDIENTS
1¼ pounds (568 g) fresh ramen noodles
8 cups (2 L) warm ramen broth (see step 1, page 99)

OTHER STUFF
Pasta pot with strainer

HOW TO
1. Fill the pasta pot with water and season with salt until it tastes like seawater. Bring to a boil over high heat. Cook the ramen for 2 to 4 minutes, to your taste.

2. Transfer the noodles to the bowls and toss with the fixings. Add the broth and stir to prevent clumping.

I heard you, Chef. I need to pick two veggies for my ramen bowl.

noodlecat

Roasted Chicken Ramen

For me, a roast chicken is incredibly satisfying. Whether you buy a chicken from a rotisserie or grocery store in your neighborhood or roast it yourself, you have a great meal and leftovers that you can turn into chicken salad and bones and skin to turn into broth. All from one bird that's the perfect size for a small family. This is our ramen-ized version of good old chicken soup.

INGREDIENTS

- 2 cups (220 g) shredded cooked chicken
- 1 recipe Roasted Chicken Ramen Broth (recipe follows, page 104)
- ½ cup (55 g) diced tofu
- 3 tablespoons (45 g) shiro miso
- 2 tablespoons (30 ml) oaked soy sauce
- 1 tablespoon (14 g) salted butter
- 1½ pounds (680 g) ramen noodles
- 6 sheets dried kombu
- 1 tablespoon (8 g) sesame seeds
- ¼ cup (25 g) sliced scallion
- 1 teaspoon bonito flakes
- 1 recipe 6½-Minute Eggs (recipe follows)

OTHER STUFF

Pasta pot with strainer
Two small saucepans
Large saucepan
Serving bowls

HOW TO

1. Fill a large pot with water and season with salt until it tastes like seawater. Bring to a boil over high heat.

2. In a small saucepan, combine the shredded chicken and just enough ramen broth to cover it. Warm over low heat.

3. In a separate small saucepan, combine the tofu with just enough ramen broth to cover it. Warm over low heat.

4. In the large saucepan, combine the remaining broth with the shiro miso, soy sauce, and butter. Warm over low heat.

5. Blanch the ramen noodles in the boiling water for 50 seconds for dried noodles, 3 minutes for fresh noodles, or 5 minutes for fresh-frozen noodles. Rinse the noodles under running hot water to remove traces of alkaline. Divide noodles among 6 bowls, divide the broth among the bowls, and stir immediately to prevent clumping.

6. Serve with the chicken, tofu, kombu, sesame seeds, scallions, bonito flakes and eggs for garnishing.

YIELD: 6 servings

It's easy to use dried kombu (seaweed) as a garnish or in a salad. Just soak it in water overnight, drain, and slice into long, thin strips.

Chef Says

Roasted Chicken Ramen Broth

INGREDIENTS

- 1 cup (70 g) dried shiitake mushrooms
- 2 sheets dried kombu
- 1 onion, sliced
- 1 carrot, sliced
- 1 head garlic, peeled
- ¼ cup (24 g) sliced ginger
- 1 gallon (4 L) water
- 1 roasted chicken, bones and skin only

OTHER STUFF

Large saucepan

HOW TO

In a large saucepan, combine the shiitakes, kombu, onion, carrot, garlic, ginger, water, and chicken bones and skin and simmer over medium-low heat for at least 4 hours. Strain the stock.

YIELD: 2 quarts (2 L)

6½-Minute Eggs

These eggs are cooked for exactly 6 minutes and 30 seconds, which cooks the white and leaves the yolk runny and delicious.

INGREDIENTS

- 6 eggs
- Ice

OTHER STUFF

Medium saucepan
Medium bowl
Kitchen timer

HOW TO

1. Bring a saucepan of salted water to a boil over high heat. Fill the bowl with water and ice to make an ice bath.

2. Add the eggs to the boiling water and set the timer for 6 minutes and 30 seconds. Remove the eggs from the boiling water and place them in the ice bath for 1 minute.

3. Peel the eggs.

YIELD: 6 eggs

Noodlecat in Japan

If you lived in Japan, you might want to eat noodles every day. If you can't go to Japan, it's time for a family trip to the Asian grocery store. See if you can pick out some of the most popular noodles on the shelf.

Soba noodles are the ones that look like flat spaghetti. They are usually a light brown or brown-gray color from the buckwheat they are made with. Udon is thicker and the noodles are white. Ramen comes in all kinds of different shapes and lengths. It can even be curly. You'll be able to tell which ones are ramen by the yellowish color.

In Japan, noodles are popular year-round. In summer noodles such as soba and udon are served cold with a dipping sauce, and in cold weather, the Japanese eat a lot of hot soups with noodles, such as ramen. There are so many different types of ramen that you could eat a different soup at every meal for a week—or forever, if you think about all the different toppings you could add. Ramen is served with a spoon and chopsticks, so you can eat every last bite.

One more thing: In Japan, it's not rude to slurp your noodles. Slurping loudly means the noodles are delicious and it helps cool them off. Slurrrppp!

Tonkatsu Ramen

Making the perfect tonkatsu is a life's work for most ramen masters: Legends are told of chefs who hand crack all the pork bones or keep a master mother broth for decades, reserving some from each batch to start the next. You can take this recipe that seriously, if you want. Or you can just think about it as a fun kitchen project and a delicious dinner.

INGREDIENTS

1½ pounds (680 g) fresh ramen noodles

2 quarts (2 L) Pork Bomb Broth (recipe follows, page 108)

3 tablespoons (45 g) shiro miso

2 cups (220 g) shredded pork shoulder (reserved from Pork Bomb Broth)

½ cup (55 g) diced tofu

¼ cup (25 g) sliced scallion

6 sheets dried kombu

1 tablespoon (8 g) sesame seeds

1 teaspoon bonito flakes

1 recipe 6½-Minute Eggs (page 104)

1 tablespoon (14 g) salted butter or pork fat

OTHER STUFF

Pasta pot with strainer

Serving bowls

Whisk

HOW TO

1. Fill the pasta pot with water and season with salt until it tastes like seawater. Bring to a boil over high heat. Cook the ramen for 2 to 4 minutes, to your taste.

2. Divide the broth among 6 bowls. Divide the shiro miso among the bowls and whisk into the broth. Divide the noodles among the bowls and stir immediately to prevent clumping.

3. Serve with the pork shoulder, tofu, scallion, kombu, sesame seeds, bonito flakes, eggs, and butter for garnishing.

YIELD: 6 servings

What's the best part about ramen? The garnishes, of course! I love kombu (it's seaweed and it's awesome!) and 6½-Minute Eggs. What are your favorites?

noodlecat

Pork Bomb Broth

This recipe requires more time and love than some of the others. It can take more than a day and a half, but the end result is so worth it!

INGREDIENTS

- ½ cup (40 g) dried mushroom powder
- 2 tablespoons (10 g) five-spice powder
- ¼ cup (72 g) kosher salt
- 2 tablespoons (30 g) brown sugar
- 1 tablespoon (7 g) paprika
- 2 pounds (908 g) bone-in pork shoulder
- 1 cup (96 g) sliced ginger
- 2 Vidalia onions, sliced
- 2 heads garlic, sliced
- 1 pig trotter, sliced crosswise
- 1 pound (454 g) meaty chicken bones (wings, drumsticks, neck, etc.)

OTHER STUFF

Small bowl
Baking sheet or grilling basket
Large roasting pan with lid

HOW TO

1. Combine the dried mushroom powder, five-spice powder, salt, brown sugar, and paprika in a small bowl. Rub the spice mixture onto the pork shoulder.

WAIT! Place the meat on a platter, add the spice rub, and cover with plastic wrap, allowing the meat to absorb the flavors of the rub. Refrigerate it for 4 to 24 hours, turning the meat occasionally.

2. Preheat the broiler. Spread the ginger, onions, and garlic on a baking sheet and char under the broiler or place in a grilling basket and char on the grill.

3. Turn the oven down to 275°F (140°C, or gas mark 1). Rinse the pig trotter in hot water for 5 minutes. Rinse the chicken bones in hot water for 5 minutes.

4. In the large roasting pan, layer the chicken bones, then the pig trotter, and then the pork shoulder. Add enough water to cover the bones, and then cover the pan. Roast low and slow for 6 hours.

5. When the meat is done roasting, remove from the oven and let cool. Remove the bone from the pork shoulder. Return the bone to the roasting pan. Shred the pork shoulder with two forks and reserve for another use, refrigerated and covered with some liquid from the roasting pan. Strain the liquid and add back to the roasting pan.

6. Transfer the roasting pan to the stove top. Add the charred ginger, onions, and garlic to the strained liquid. Simmer over low heat for at least 8 hours, adding water as needed to maintain a volume of about 1 gallon (4 L).

YIELD: 1 gallon (4 L)

Noodlecat in Korea

The Korean kitchen has all kinds of noodles made from cool things you won't see almost anywhere else, such as acorns, kudzu, sweet potato, and seaweed. Some of the noodles are made by rolling out dough and cutting into long strips with a knife, but other noodles are pulled, spun, and stretched by hand, almost like a pizza maker throwing the dough in the air. It's so cool to watch.

There's a special noodle dish in Korean culture called *janchi guksu* that's eaten at weddings or birthdays. It's soupy with long, thin noodles and a fried egg on top. They eat it on special occasions because long noodles mean longevity. It's a wish for a long marriage and a long life.

On Black Day, an unofficial holiday celebrated on April 14 each year, single people get together to eat jajangmyeon, a dish of thick noodles with black bean sauce. The day is associated with Valentine's Day and White Day. Those who do not receive gifts enjoy the gift of noodles.

Chapter 8

Gluten-Free Friends

Amelia's family is from Trentino, the northern part of Italy. The terrain can be a challenge, as can the altitude, so almost all their pastas are based on farro or kamut.

We got to know these pastas on our trips there, and as Americans have become more aware of gluten and gluten-free recipes, we've started serving more gluten-free noodles, such as farro pasta, at our restaurants. From the beginning we knew we wanted to do more than just accommodate dietary restrictions such as vegan, vegetarian, and gluten free. We wanted to embrace them. There are so many options, in so many different cuisines. Some of our favorites are rice noodles from Vietnam and Thailand, Korean-style rice cakes, and Asian rice paper. At our house, rice paper means it's time for a Family Rock-and-Summer-Roll Celebration (page 119).

Farro with Walnuts and Pork

Farro has recently become a popular grain in America, but in Trentino noodles have been made with farro for years. It's not about dietary restrictions or trends; it's about using what grows in the region. Classic Italian recipes such as this one let farro shine.

INGREDIENTS

- 4 tablespoons (56 g) salted butter, divided
- 1 Vidalia onion, diced
- 1 pound (454 g) farro linguine
- ½ cup (55 g) finely diced smoked pancetta
- 1 sprig rosemary
- ¼ tablespoon finely crushed juniper
- ¼ tablespoon finely crushed allspice
- ¼ cup (30 g) chopped black walnuts
- ¼ cup (60 ml) dry red wine
- 1 tablespoon (15 ml) buttermilk
- ¼ cup (25 g) grated Parmesan cheese
- 1 tablespoon (15 ml) cold-pressed, extra-virgin olive oil
- ¼ cup (25 g) toasted bread crumbs

OTHER STUFF

Sauté pan
Bowl
Pasta pot with strainer

HOW TO

1. In the sauté pan over low heat, melt 3 tablespoons (42 g) of the butter and add the onion, cooking until soft, about 30 to 45 minutes. Transfer the caramelized onions to a bowl and reserve.

2. Fill the pasta pot with water and season with salt until it tastes like seawater. Bring to a boil over high heat. Add the farro noodles, stirring to prevent the noodles from sticking to the bottom of the pan, and cooked until al dente, about 10 to 12 minutes. Drain the noodles and reserve ¼ cup (60 ml) of the pasta water.

3. In the sauté pan over low heat, cook the pancetta until the fat is rendered. Add the rosemary, juniper, allspice, and black walnuts and cook over medium heat until the walnuts are toasted. Add the wine and continue to cook over medium heat until the pan is dry. Add the caramelized onions, buttermilk, cooked farro noodles, and the pasta water. (Start with 2 tablespoons [30 ml] pasta water and add more as needed.) Simmer until the sauce comes together, 2 to 3 minutes. Remove from the heat.

4. Remove the rosemary sprig and fold in the remaining 1 tablespoon (14 g) butter and the cheese. Drizzle with the olive oil and garnish with the bread crumbs.

YIELD: 4 servings

You can always experiment with a recipe if you don't like or don't have a certain ingredient. But remember: Bacon is very different from pancetta, so if you can't find smoked pancetta (*pancetta affumicato* in Italian), a good substitution would be ¼ cup (25 g) diced regular pancetta and ¼ cup (25 g) diced bacon, for the smokiness.

Chef Says

Pho Noodle Soup

It's all about the broth, baby. This started as an experiment after we visited a Vietnamese restaurant with the kids and saw the big pot of pho broth simmering in the kitchen. I love to make this broth because you can let it cook for a whole day. The anticipation for the soup builds as you smell it simmering away. I love that. I got that from my mother and my grandmother: The second you walk in the front door, you should know there's food on the stove to greet you.

INGREDIENTS

- 4 beef shank bones, sliced
- 2 Vidalia onions, halved
- 1 cup (96 g) ¼-inch (6 mm) thick sliced ginger
- 10 star anise
- 6 allspice
- 4 whole cloves
- 1 stick cinnamon
- 6 tablespoons (90 ml) fish sauce, plus more for drizzling
- 1 teaspoon brown sugar
- 1 to 1½ pounds (454 to 680 g) rice vermicelli
- 1 tablespoon (6 g) sliced scallion
- ½ cup (16 g) chopped Vietnamese herbs (choose your favorites: Thai basil, purple basil, Chinese chives, shiso leaf, mint, cilantro, chrysanthemum greens, mustard leaves)
- ½ cup (55 g) diced tofu
- 1 tablespoon (15 ml) lime juice
- 1 tablespoon (15 ml) sweet soy sauce
- 1 tablespoon (15 ml) chili sauce

OTHER STUFF

2-gallon (2 L) saucepan
Pasta pot with strainer
Serving bowls

HOW TO

1. Rinse the bones well with hot water. Using your broiler or grill, char the onions and bones.

2. In the large saucepan, combine the ginger, star anise, allspice, cloves, cinnamon, fish sauce, and brown sugar. Fill with water and simmer over low heat, skimming regularly.

WAIT! Simmer the stock for at least 8 hours. At the Sawyer house, we cook it overnight. Strain before using.

3. Fill the pasta pot with water and season with salt until it tastes like seawater. Bring to a boil over high heat. Add the vermicelli noodles and stir for 2 minutes to prevent sticking. Cook for another 2 to 4 minutes, until al dente.

4. Divide the noodles among 4 bowls, cover with the broth, and add the scallion, herbs, and tofu. Drizzle with the lime juice, sweet soy sauce, chili sauce, and fish sauce to your taste.

YIELD: 4 servings

> This is the only recipe in the book that calls for beef bones. I don't use them a lot in my cooking, but with pho, it's absolutely essential.
>
> *Chef Says*

Lulu's K-Style Rice Cakes

You can think of this as a Korean, gluten-free gnocchi. We sometimes fry them after blanching and call them rice fries or rice tots. The cooking technique is similar to a classic gnocchi recipe, but it also has a lot in common with a stir-fry. The recipe moves quickly, so have all the ingredients ready to go before you heat up that wok.

INGREDIENTS

- 1 pound (454 g) Asian rice cakes (available at most Asian markets)
- 1 to 2 tablespoons (15 to 30 ml) vegetable oil
- 4 ounces (112 g) cooked brisket
- 3 cloves garlic
- 1 tablespoon (8 g) smashed ginger
- 1 teaspoon sesame seeds
- ¼ cup (25 g) sliced scallion
- 1 teaspoon ground black pepper
- 2 tablespoons (30 ml) soy sauce
- ¼ cup (60 g) gochujang Korean chili paste
- Salt and pepper, to taste
- 10 leaves lettuce (choose your favorite: butter, Bibb, or Boston lettuce)
- ½ cup (8 g) chopped cilantro, for garnish
- ½ cup (48 g) chopped mint, for garnish
- 1 cup (100 g) kimchi, for garnish
- 1 Asian pear, diced
- 1 cup (90 g) thinly sliced napa cabbage
- 1 lemon, cut into wedges

OTHER STUFF

- Pasta pot with strainer
- Sauté pan or wok
- Serving tray

HOW TO

1. Fill the pot with water and season with salt until it tastes like seawater. Bring to a boil over high heat. Cook the rice cakes until cooked through, about 12 minutes.

2. While the rice cakes are cooking, heat the oil in the sauté pan or wok over high heat. Strain the rice cakes well and add them to the wok. Sear them well on one side without disturbing. Add the brisket, garlic, ginger, sesame seeds, scallion, and black pepper on top of the rice cakes. When the cakes are light golden brown on one side, 1 to 2 minutes, you can start to stir. When the cakes are evenly browned on the other side, 1 to 2 minutes, add the soy sauce and gochujang and stir until the rice cakes are coated. Season with salt and pepper to taste.

3. Lay the lettuce leaves on a serving tray. Top with the rice cakes and garnish with the chopped herbs, kimchi, Asian pear, napa cabbage, and lemon wedges.

YIELD: 4 servings

How to Throw a Family Rock-and-Summer-Roll Celebration

You can tell we like the idea of a party: We like interactive food and lots of choices so that everyone at the table can find a flavor he or she loves—and maybe try something new. Summer rolls are just a noodle-y burrito influenced by Japanese and Chinese cuisines, with lots of tasty fillings and condiments wrapped up in steamed rice paper.

1 Prep the Fillings and Condiments

Like the Ramen Party (page 98), this Summer Roll Celebration is all about the prep.

Vermicelli

When cooking vermicelli, stirring the noodles for the first 2 minutes keeps everything from sticking. Reserve the hot water. You'll use it to steam the rice papers in step 2.

INGREDIENTS
1   pound (454 g) rice vermicelli

OTHER STUFF
Pasta pot with strainer

HOW TO
Fill the pot with water and season with salt until it tastes like seawater. Bring to a boil over high heat. Add the vermicelli noodles and stir for 2 minutes to prevent sticking. Cook for another 2 to 4 minutes, until al dente. Strain, reserving the water for step 2.

YIELD: 4 servings

Tasty Tofu

The trick here is to add just enough liquid to coat the tofu, but not so much that it leaves a puddle of liquid in the bowl.

INGREDIENTS

1 package (14 ounces, or 392 g) tofu, cut into strips
1 to 2 tablespoons (15 to 30 ml) lime juice
1 to 2 tablespoons (15 to 30 ml) soy sauce
1 to 2 tablespoons (15 to 30 ml) sesame oil

OTHER STUFF
Bowl

HOW TO

Combine all the ingredients and toss gently to coat the tofu.

Avocado and Lime

Lime and avocado are a great flavor combination. It's a bonus that the citrus prevents the avocado from turning brown quickly.

INGREDIENTS

1 lime
1 cup (145 g) chopped avocado

OTHER STUFF
Microplane
Bowl

HOW TO

Using the microplane, zest the lime into the bowl. Cut the lime and squeeze the juice into the zest. Fold in the avocado.

YIELD: 1 cup (145 g)

Other Filling and Condiment Ideas

Usually this party is an excuse to clean out the fridge and use the last of the black beans or that leftover peanut sauce.

INGREDIENTS

1 cup (250 g) cooked black beans
1 cup (200 g) poached shrimp
2 cups (140 g) sliced herb and lettuce mix (choose your favorites: Bibb, mint, cilantro)
½ cup (50 g) sliced scallion
¼ cup (25 g) crispy shallots (available at Asian markets)
¼ cup (25 g) shredded carrot
¼ cup (25 g) shredded daikon
¼ cup (25 g) pickled ginger
¼ cup (60 ml) Crushed Peanut Dipping Sauce (page 27)
¼ cup (60 ml) soy sauce
¼ cup (60 g) miso sauce
¼ cup (60 ml) fish sauce

OTHER STUFF
Bowls

HOW TO

Arrange all the ingredients in bowls on the table. Along with the vermicelli, tofu, and avocado, these will be the fillings for the summer rolls.

2 Steam the Rice Papers

It's easy to steam the rice paper rounds with an inexpensive perforated screen that you can pick up at most Asian markets.

INGREDIENTS
1   package (12 ounces, or 336 g) rice paper rounds

OTHER STUFF
Perforated screen or colander
Pasta pot with lid with some hot water reserved
      from step 1

HOW TO
Insert the perforated screen or colander on top of the pasta pot, making sure the water doesn't reach above the basket. Working one at a time, place a rice paper round on the screen, cover the pot with a lid, and steam each rice paper round until soft, about 30 seconds.

3 Roll!

If you've ever rolled up a burrito, you know how to make a summer roll. Put your favorite fillings and condiments in the middle of the rice paper round. You don't want to make it too full or it will be tough to roll. Fold the left and right edges toward the middle and then, starting at the bottom, roll the rice paper over the fillings.

Chapter 9

You Can Do That with Noodles?

We've stuffed, baked, sauced, and slurped all kinds of noodles in this book. So what is left to do with noodles? Lots! Once you get to know your noodles, you learn that you can serve noodles as an appetizer, and you can serve them in salad. You can serve them as a sandwich (really!) and even as a cold remedy. The best thing about noodles is that there's no limit to the fun you can have in the kitchen with your family.

Grilled Ramen and Cheese

This is a really fun way to reinterpret ramen noodles. I like to think about these cuties almost like potato latkes, gently assembled and easy to pick up. At Noodlecat, we serve this with creamy tomato soup mixed with miso, but I also love it with onion dip or hummus.

INGREDIENTS
16 ounces (454 g) fresh ramen noodles
 1 tablespoon (14 g) salted butter
 1 bunch scallions, sliced
 1 clove garlic, smashed
 1 teaspoon paprika
    Salt and pepper, to taste
 2 cups (225 g) shredded aged cheddar cheese
 ½ cup (50 g) grated Parmesan cheese

OTHER STUFF
Pasta pot with strainer
Large bowl
9 x 13-inch (23 x 33 cm) baking dish
Parchment paper
Soup cans
Cutting board
Panini press

HOW TO
1. Fill the pot with water and season with salt until it tastes like seawater. Bring to a boil over high heat. Cook the ramen noodles for 8 minutes. Strain them but do not rinse them; you want that extra starch.

2. In the large bowl, combine the hot ramen noodles, butter, scallions, garlic, paprika, and salt and pepper. Allow the ramen to cool slightly, and then fold in the cheeses. You want to stir gently, but it's okay if the noodles tear a little.

3. Line a baking pan with lightly greased parchment paper. Transfer the ramen mixture to the pan and spread evenly to form a ramen cake. The cake should be 1½ to 2½-inches (3.8 to 6.4 cm) thick. Top the mixture with another piece of lightly greased parchment paper. Place the soup cans on top of the parchment paper to compress the cake.

WAIT! Refrigerate the ramen cake for at least 2 hours and up to 24 hours.

4. Once the ramen cake has cooled, turn it out onto a cutting board, still layered with the parchment. Cut the cake, still in the parchment paper, into 3-inch (7.5 cm) squares.

5. Remove the parchment paper and press each ramen cake in a panini press at medium heat until golden brown, about 10 minutes.

YIELD: 4 appetizer servings

Stracciatella alla Romana

Stracciatella is one of those Italian words used for a vast variety of food descriptors, from the milky filling of the classic burrata to gelato in which warm chocolate is drizzled into the freezing cold churning gelato base to pasta sheets torn by hand to this soul-satisfying version of Roman egg drop soup, which is a favorite cold remedy.

INGREDIENTS

- 4 large fresh eggs
- ¼ cup (32 g) semolina flour
- 6 tablespoons (36 g) grated Parmesan cheese
- 1 tablespoon (15 ml) cold-pressed, extra-virgin olive oil, divided
- 6 cups (1410 ml) Roasted Chicken Broth (page 104)
  Salt and pepper, to taste
- 2 tablespoons (14 g) finely sliced spinach
- 2 tablespoons (8 g) finely sliced parsley

OTHER STUFF

Stand mixer (optional)

Medium saucepan with a cover

It's easy to adapt this recipe. Instead of the spinach and parsley, simmer the broth with smashed garlic cloves for a comforting cold remedy, replace the semolina with all-purpose flour for a homey dumpling, or go for luxury with the addition of white truffles. In New York there is an American/Mexican late-night version beloved by cooks in the best kitchens called *sopa d'ajo*, or garlic soup. Add a simple, shredded poached egg with an insane amount of pulverized garlic and serve with fiery chipotle and jalapeño pico de gallo.

Chef Says

HOW TO

1. In the stand mixer or bowl, combine the eggs, semolina, Parmesan, and 2 teaspoons (10 ml) of the olive oil. Mix by hand or at medium speed for 7 minutes.

2. In the saucepan, bring the broth to a boil and season with salt and pepper. Add the spinach and parsley and simmer, covered, for 2 minutes. Pipe in the egg mixture slowly, and simmer, covered, for 2 more minutes. Garnish with the remaining 1 teaspoon (5 ml) olive oil.

YIELD: 4 servings

Combine the eggs, semolina, Parmesan, and 2 teaspoons (10 ml) of the olive oil.

Mix well.

Transfer the mixture to a plastic bag for piping into the simmering broth.

Noodlecat in Italy

Long skinny noodles, short fat noodles, fresh noodles, dry noodles, round noodles, square noodles, butterfly-shaped noodles—Italy has them all. It's the first place we think of when we think of pasta. Italians eat more than 60 pounds (27 kg) of pasta per person per year, and Italy has more than 300 different types of pasta (and 1,300 different names for those pastas).

If you tour around Italy, you learn that each of those pastas comes from a very particular place, and every region is really proud of its pasta. Orecchiette, those little ear-shaped pastas, were invented at the "heel" of Italy in Puglia. Northern Italy created tortellini, a stuffed pasta that is supposed to look like a belly button, and farfalle pasta, the one that looks like a butterfly or a bow tie. Macaroni was born in Naples in the south and Rome is known for everyone's favorite: spaghetti!

Until the sixteenth century, Italians ate spaghetti with their fingers, but you probably shouldn't do that at the dinner table. Can you twirl your spaghetti around your fork?

Chilled Soba and Seaweed Salad

You know those bow-tie pasta salads with Italian dressing, olives, and veggies you always find at a cookout? This is a Japanese version of the typical picnic salad. It's a simple, light lunch to be enjoyed with sunlight.

INGREDIENTS

- 1 tablespoon (15 ml) sweet soy sauce
- 1 tablespoon (15 ml) soy sauce
- 1 head garlic, cloves peeled and grated
- 1 teaspoon grated ginger
- 1 lemon, zested and juiced
- 2 tablespoons (30 ml) rice wine vinegar
  Chili sauce, to taste
- 1 tablespoon (15 ml) sesame oil
- 2 tablespoons (30 ml) vegetable oil
- ½ cup (60 g) shredded carrot
- 1 pound (454 g) soba noodles
- ½ cup (48 g) sliced kombu
- 1 tablespoon (8 g) sesame seeds
- ½ cup (50 g) sliced scallion
- 1 container (4 ounces, or 112 g) sprouts (choose spicy sprouts such as horseradish, daikon, wasabi, or mustard)

OTHER STUFF

Large bowl
Whisk
Pasta pot with strainer

HOW TO

1. In the large bowl, whisk together both soy sauces, garlic, ginger, lemon zest and juice, rice wine vinegar, chili sauce, sesame oil, and vegetable oil. Add the shredded carrot and stir to combine.

WAIT! Refrigerate for 20 minutes, until the carrots are quick-pickled.

2. Fill the pot with water and season with salt until it tastes like seawater. Bring to a boil over high heat. Cook the soba noodles until slightly underdone, 5 minutes for fresh noodles, 7 minutes for dried noodles. Rinse the noodles in cold water until cooled.

3. Toss the cooled noodles with the vinaigrette, kombu, and sesame seeds.

WAIT! Let the noodles marinate in the refrigerator for 10 minutes.

4. Garnish with the scallion and sprouts.

YIELD: 4 servings

Crunchy Ramen and Apple Salad

One of the things I love about my mother-in-law is her classic salad preparations. She makes ambrosia, Waldorf, and the king: crunchy ramen salad. This is my version, with more traditional Asian flavors.

INGREDIENTS

1½ inches (3.8 cm) ginger, grated
1 head garlic, peeled
1 tablespoon (15 ml) soy sauce
2 tablespoons (30 ml) red wine vinegar
2 tart apples, peeled, cored, and cut into matchsticks
1 lemon, zested and juiced
½ head cabbage, shredded
   Salt, to taste
3 tablespoons (45 ml) grapeseed oil
1 tablespoon (14 g) Kewpie mayonnaise
2 packages (3 ounces, or 84 g) unseasoned instant ramen noodles, divided
½ cup (50 g) sliced almonds, toasted, divided
1 sheet kombu, sliced
¼ cup (25 g) crispy shallots (available at many Asian markets.)
1 bunch basil, leaves only

OTHER STUFF

Grater
3 large bowls
Whisk

HOW TO

1. Grate the ginger and garlic into a bowl, add the soy sauce and red wine vinegar, and stir to combine. In a separate bowl, toss the apples with the lemon zest and juice. In a third bowl, season the cabbage generously with salt.

WAIT! Let the ingredients in each bowl marinate for 10 minutes.

2. To finish the vinaigrette, whisk the oil and mayonnaise into the soy sauce–vinegar mixture until emulsified. Add three-quarters of the ramen noodles, three-quarters of the apples, ¼ cup (25 g) of the almonds, and all of the cabbage to the vinaigrette and toss to coat.

3. Garnish with the seaweed, remaining ¼ cup (25 g) almonds, remaining one-quarter noodles and apples, the crispy shallots, and the basil.

YIELD: 5 appetizer servings

About the Author

Chef Jonathon Sawyer is a proud Clevelander and a graduate of the Pennsylvania Institute of Culinary Arts. He began his culinary career at The Biltmore Hotel in Miami before working in New York City alongside Charlie Palmer at Kitchen 22. Chef Sawyer worked as chef de cuisine for his friend and colleague Michael Symon and then became Symon's executive chef at Parea, receiving a two-star review from the *New York Times*.

In 2007, Jonathon moved back to his hometown to pursue his dream of opening his own restaurant. Before his dream was realized, Chef Sawyer partnered with a local entrepreneur to open Bar Cento, a modern Roman enoteca in Cleveland's Ohio City neighborhood. During his tenure as chef and partner, Bar Cento received many accolades, including Northern Ohio Live's Best New Restaurant, and brought Jonathon much personal attention, earning him the Rising Star Chef award from both *Restaurant Hospitality* and *GAYOT*.

Since those days Jonathon has opened four restaurants in Cleveland including his flagship, The Greenhouse Tavern, a French- and seasonally inspired gastropub and Noodlecat, a mash-up noodlehouse focusing on local ingredients, sustainability, and the best ramen Cleveland has ever seen. Both restaurants are certified by the Green Restaurant Association. The Greenhouse Tavern has earned many awards including Best New Restaurant in the United States by *Bon Appétit* magazine. Jonathon Sawyer was also honored as a recipient of *Food & Wine* magazine's Best New Chef award in 2010. In 2013, Jonathon became a finalist for the James Beard Award's Best Chef: Great Lakes. He has also made several national television appearances including *Iron Chef America, Dinner Impossible, Unique Eats*, and *The Best Thing I Ever Ate.*

In 2011 he started the Tavern Vinegar Company. He can often be found in the cellar of his century-old home where he ferments more than 300 gallons (1136 L) of single-origin and blended wine, beer, and malt vinegars for the restaurants and for retail sale.

In 2012, Jonathon opened a second Noodlecat location in Cleveland's Historical West Side Market and followed that opening with a brand new concept, "Sawyer's Street Frites," in the Cleveland Browns' Stadium just in time the 2012–2013 football season and opened another stadium establishment, SeeSaw Pretzel Shoppe in Quicken Loans Arena.

His newest restaurant is Northern Italian–inspired Trentina. When Jonathon is not in the kitchen, he is surrounded by his family, his wife Amelia, son Catcher, daughter Louisiana, dogs Potato and Vito, and chickens Acorn, Bunny, Ginger, Trout, Bear, and Squid. Jonathon is a tireless supporter of the green movement, local agriculture, and sustainable businesses both in Northeast Ohio and around the country.

About the Photographer

Kate Lewis is a New York City– and Ohio-based food and travel photographer and stylist. Over the years she has held every restaurant position from hostess, server, and bartender to chocolatier, barista, and cook. Her culinary background and fine-arts training combined with her passion for food prompted her to begin shooting portraits for renowned chefs and highly stylized photographs. Kate's photography and styling has worked with national publications like *Food & Wine*, *VegNews*, best-selling authors, and more than ten cookbooks. Follow Kate's everyday adventures on Instagram and Twitter (@_Kate_Lewis), and visit her website at kk-lewis.com.

Acknowledgments

This book would not have been possible without the support and encouragement of my wife, Amelia, and our kids Catcher and Louisiana. Thank you for the guidance and professional advice of editors Mary Ann Hall, Jonathan Simcosky, and the entire Noodle Kids' team at Quarto Publishing Group, and for the stellar photography by Kate Lewis—our chickens look fabulous! To my committed administrative and culinary team Brian Goodman, Tessa Earhart, and Jessica Lubrano: Thank you for your dedication.

Further Reading

Asian Dumplings: Mastering Gyoza, Spring Rolls, Samosas, and More, Andrea Nguyen. Ten Speed Press, 2009.

Grand Livre De Cuisine: Alain Ducasse's Culinary Encyclopedia, Alain Ducasse. Ducasse Books, 2009.

Ivan Ramen: Love, Obsession, and Recipes from Tokyo's Most Unlikely Noodle Joint, Ivan Orkin. Ten Speed Press, 2013.

Japanese Farm Foods, Nancy Singleton Hachisu. Andrews McMeel Publishing, 2012.

Japanese Hot Pots; Comforting One-Pot Meals, Ono Tadashi and Salat Harris. Ten Speed Press, 2009.

Larousse Gastronomique: The World's Greatest Culinary Encyclopedia, Completely Revised and Updated, Larousse Librairie. Clarkson Potter, 2009.

L'Atelier of Joel Robuchon: The Artistry of a Master Chef and His Proteges, Patricia Wells, Joel Robuchon, and Herve Amiard. Houghton Mifflin Hourte, 1997.

Made in Italy: Food and Stories, Giorgio Locatelli. Ecco, 2007.

Molto Batali: Simple Family Meals from My Home to Yours, Mario Batali. Ecco, 2011.

Molto Italiano: 327 Simple Italian Recipes to Cook at Home, Mario Batali. Ecco, 2005.

Momofuku, David Chang and Peter Meehan. Clarkson Potter, 2013.

Noodle, Terry Durak. Soma Books, 2002.

Noodles: The New Way, Sri Owen. Villard, 2000.

Pasta: Classic and Contemporary Pasta, Risotto,Crespelle, and Polenta Recipes (at Home with The Cul), The Culinary Institute of America. Houghton Mifflin Harcourt, 2013.

Potsticker Chronicles: America's Favorite Chinese Recipes, Stuart Chang Berman. Houghton Mifflin Harcourt, 2004.

Rustic Italian Food, Marc Vetri and David Joachim. Ten Speed Press, 2011.

SPQR: Modern Italian Food and Wine, Shelley Lindgren, Matthew Accarrino, and Kate Leahy. Ten Speed Press, 2012.

Takashi's Noodles, Takshi Yagihashi and Salat Harris. Ten Speed Press, 2009.

The Complete Robuchan, Joel Robuchan. Knopf, 2008.

The Geometry of Pasta, Caz Hildebrand and Jacob Kenedy. Quirk Books, 2010.

The Mozza Cookbook: Recipes from Los Angeles' Favorite Italian Restaraunt and Pizzareia, Nancy Silverton, Matt Molina, and Carolynn Carreno. Knopf, 2011.

Further Reading For Kids

Kids Cook French, Claudine and Jacques Pépin
ISBN: 1-59253-953-6

Kitchen Science Lab for Kids, Liz Lee Heinecke
ISBN: 1-59253-925-3

Gardening Lab for Kids, Renata Fossen Brown
ISBN: 1-59253-904-8

Baking with Kids, Leah Brooks
ISBN: 1-59253-977-2

Cupcake Decorating Lab, Bridget Thibeault
ISBN: 1-59253-831-7

Index

Recipe Notes